Dark Horse Candidate

Other Books by Dale Christensen

Patriot's Path (2014)
– a plan for our future

Guide to Greatness (2014)
– inspiration to bring out the greatness in everyone

A Disciple's Journey (2014)
– spiritual perspective and religious background

Thoughts in Verse (2014)
– uplifting poetry

10 Secrets To Speaking English (2001)
– method of helping people to speak a new language

Out of Print:

The Shopping Center Acquisition Handbook (1984)
– complete process and documentation

Turning the Hearts Vol. I-IV *(1982)*
– family history from earliest ancestors to marriage

History of the Church in Peru (1991)
– selective personal and general highlights

Entrepreneur Guide: The Ultimate Business & Learning Experience
(2001)
– textbook for MBA course

Teaching Improvement Program
– USTC MBA Program & Business School (2001)
– training for MBA professors

Dark Horse Candidate

BY

DALE CHRISTENSEN

"I pledge allegiance to
the Constitution of the United States of America
and to the flag and to the Republic for which it stands,
one nation under God, indivisible, with liberty and justice for all."

Dark Horse Candidate

Published by:
Dale Christensen
Books@Dale2016.com

Cover design: Matt Christensen and Rachael Gibson
Editing Assistance: Jan Jackson and Susan Allen Myers

Library of Congress, Catalog-in-Publication Data

ISBN
Hardback: 978-1-942345-00-8
Softback: 978-1-942345-01-5
eBook: 978-1-942345-02-2
Audio: 978-1-942345-03-9

Printed in the United States of America
Year of first printing: 2014

Dedication

This book is dedicated to my children, grandchildren, and to all who hope and pray for a brighter future.

The Pilgrims gave us an American dream. The Founding Fathers gave us a new nation. The generations that followed gave us legacy, legend, and promise through growth and struggle.

My grandparents' generation gave us a values-based culture. My parents' generation gave us prosperity, unlimited opportunity, and the opportunity to bless the world as never before. My generation is about to give you debt, conflict, and moral decay.

I will do everything in my power to give you the brighter future you hope for and deserve. In doing so, let me just give you the two following definitions:

- **Democracy**: Rule by the *majority* of the people. In the United States, laws are NOT made by a majority vote of the citizens.

- **Republic**: Rule by *representatives* of the people. The people elect *representatives* by a majority vote. Then the representatives make the laws. The word "Democracy" is NOT in the Constitution.

Acknowledgements

Love and gratitude to my mother, Esther Christensen, who planted the first seeds of patriotism in my heart. And to my wife, Mary-Jo, for being my most candid critic and strongest supporter. Appreciation and applause to Chris Heimerdinger who helped me organize, draft, critique, and edit this manuscript. Thank you also to Jan Jackson and Susan Myers for editing and making valuable recommendations.

Vision

To believe in something so strong that the vision can be revealed in one's mind is indeed faith! To work and bring that vision into reality is also a purpose of mortality; yesterday a dream, today an ideal, tomorrow a reality! Planning and preparation are keys to progress. To be prepared allows us to look up and contribute to the world, instead of merely watching our feet each step of the way. Life is the process of finding out who we really are and becoming whatever we can conceive. It is a journey, not a destination. At the end of our travels, the most exciting thing is not to recall the journey, but to contemplate and begin anew to explore the horizons we've discovered along the way.

—Dale Christensen

Table of Contents

Introduction

Hello, America! I am Dale Christensen, and I'm a candidate to be President of the United States. My story is unique, and my message is true. This book will serve to introduce me as a messenger, and it will outline my message. I will present a clear plan to get our nation back on the right path. I don't claim to be the perfect candidate or to have all the answers, but I do know that if we are united, and if we rely on God's help, we will be blessed and protected as a nation.

Every alert citizen and foreign observer knows the United States of America is at a vital crossroad and decisive moment in history. We are at a point in time when the choice of the next President and subsequent decisions and legislation will either bring us to our knees or revive our strength and vitality.

Now is the time for us to rise up and make our place in history. It is for you as individuals, and for us as a nation, to change the course of history. Such change only comes about by faith, work, and sacrifice. These are results of study, reason, choice, and wise decision making.

So, before I ask for your vote, I invite you to read this book and become familiar with who I am and what I stand for. Become acquainted with me as a messenger and then understand my message. Decide for yourself if I am worthy to be your candidate. Choose for yourself to act on what I am inviting you to do. I am not asking you to just follow me, send me money, and vote for me. Far more importantly, I am asking you to join with me in a great campaign. I'm asking you to make a pledge to preserve and protect the Constitution of the United States of America. I am asking you to help save the moral, economic, and political soul of our nation.

I have no ambition to use the office of President to get gain or accumulate power for me or anyone else. I do have a burning desire to pull down those in power who make themselves rich off the people they should be serving. I do have the ambition to dissolve their imbedded political career status and to shrink the bureaucracy they are creating to perpetuate their own importance.

Our Founding Fathers knew, as did the original Roman Empire builders, that professional or perpetual politicians are quickly blinded by their status and quickly get imbedded in corruption. Their service turns to personal survival, which is only preserved through favors for friends, colleagues, and special interests. They become obligated to a few, when they should be providing principled service to all the people. America must root out *fixture politicians.*

Regardless of age, sex, race, religion, political persuasion or lifestyle, I invite every American to join with me in this campaign for truth and liberty. I am inviting you as an individual. I am inviting you as a family, community, state, and nation. I am inviting you to become reacquainted with the Declaration of Independence and the U.S. Constitution. I am challenging you to read them and re-read them. Share these ideas with others, and discuss what you have learned.

I invite you to become reacquainted with our Founding Fathers and our majestic history as a nation. Join with them and join with me to make a difference for today and for future generations. We are not alone! We can and must prevail in getting out of debt, in restoring the balance of power, and in securing sound reason for law.

To the retired, I invite you to embrace your roots, get up off your sofa, the comfort of your lawn chair or golf cart to join our army of youth, X and Y generations and baby boomers and make a difference while there's still time. To those still working, I invite you to balance your after-hours attention from relaxation, sport, or vacation to unite with others in public awareness, action, and service. To the youth, I challenge you to prepare yourselves to be the future leaders of our nation. Learn now and learn well whom to trust and what principles you can build on in order to stay on the right course.

Each of you can pass this book on to a friend or neighbor or grab a dozen of them to give out, even if your friends don't share your political views. If you do it with kindness and respect, they will appreciate your gesture. If you are sincere in your approach, I promise you that all parties will benefit from whatever follows.

Each of you can call a friend on the telephone, write a letter, send an e-mail, text, or tweet to all your friends and contacts. Tell them about the "dark horse candidate" and share any part of my message that resonates with you. Share a message of confidence in the Constitution. Share a message of hope in the future. Share a message of warning about where we have strayed and how we can get back on track. Do whatever you are impressed to do, but do it. Do it now.

PIVOTAL POINT IN HISTORY

There is urgency, great urgency. Time is of the essence. If we miss this window of opportunity, the doors of freedom may close. It all depends on what you want. Be careful of what you want, because you will most likely get it. Be careful of what you do or don't do, because you must live with the consequences.

America must choose leaders based on character, honesty, and integrity. We all have human faults and failings, but it is not enough to choose a President just based on being intelligent, attractive, and dynamic. Now, at this pivotal time, America needs someone uniquely qualified to change the course of history. I have undertaken this urgent mission to help our nation regain its balance at this critical tipping point.

This is a daunting task which will bring skepticism, ridicule, and persecution. But in spite of this pending hostility, I accept this responsibility with the knowledge that no worthy cause has ever prevailed without such opposition. I have chosen to sacrifice my quiet and enjoyable private life to serve, in spite of the many risks it may pose to me and those I love. I do this as a duty and for my love of God, liberty and country.

Success in preserving the U.S. Constitution and personal liberty will only be realized through faith in God, faith in ourselves, and faith in one another. It will only happen if we share a common vision, and if we do what is necessary. "Where there is no vision, the people perish" (Proverbs 29). As our vision, we must recognize the Constitution and what it represents. We must always remember that this vision came from God. The Constitution was divinely inspired, and we are free because of God's mercy and help. Without Him, we cannot prevail. With Him, we cannot fail.

Freedom and prosperity is about service, sacrifice, and loving our fellowman. It is not and was never about power, privilege, comfort, or entitlement. Over a hundred years ago, the United States began down a path of indulgence and selfishness. There have been moments of heroic unity and victory, but there has been a gradual acceptance of socialistic principles and government control. This didn't happen overnight, and it can't be fixed overnight. However, we can change our direction and repair the damage much more quickly than some might think.

My wife, children, family and friends know my strengths and my weaknesses. I have made my share of mistakes, but I declare to you, and stand before God today to declare I am ready, willing, able and worthy to represent you, to serve you, and to sacrifice for you. I promise to provide for you the right leadership, at the right time, with the right principles and tools, first and foremost being the Constitution of the United States.

Despite my weaknesses, I am confident that I am the best candidate for this presidential election. I will not focus on weaknesses of others, nor criticize their mistakes. Instead, I will focus on my message and on me as a presidential candidate. It will be for you to become informed and to choose the future of the United States of America. It is my pleasure to get acquainted and stand beside you in this great campaign. Welcome!

WEBSTER'S DEFINITION

A "dark horse candidate" is defined in Webster's dictionary as someone who is a little-known candidate or competitor, with interesting qualities and unexpected talents or abilities. The candidate is unlikely to succeed and not expected to win, but then achieves unexpected support and is nominated during the party convention as a compromise between factions in selecting a candidate.

There have been many dark horse candidates in local and state elections. However, there have been only a few for the presidency of the United States, including James K. Polk,

Abraham Lincoln, Rutherford Hayes, Warren Harding, and Jimmy Carter. Each was an underdog and nominated by their party, after many ballots, in an effort to bring the people together.

Today, America is galvanized by political dogma and opposing viewpoints. All media networks, many icons, and everyday citizens are being drawn to fragmented political factions. This polarization effect and intensity has not been as evident or as infectious since the days leading up to the Civil War. Reason and courtesy is being lost to enmity and deceit.

We must return to "value divergent opinions" that will help us bring about more effective and enduring policies founded on constitutional principles. Diversity, debate, compromise and tolerance are welcome in the public arena as long as we are all looking to the Constitution as the final arbitrator. The problems we have today are a result of leaving the Constitution behind. Poor choices have resulted in bad laws and programs around which government bureaucracies have been built. These programs and bureaucracies are now interdependent.

We must find our way back to the Constitution and correct our mistakes in order to see our way forward and move on into a brighter future. We can and must expose and confront the errors of our ways. This will not be easy. In fact, it will be very difficult and uncomfortable. However, it is possible, and together we can do it. We *can* make this happen!

Everyone will ask, "How can I be sure? How can I know who is right and what I should do?"

My answer is, "Read and study the Constitution. Then become well acquainted with the character of the candidates, what they stand for, and what they have done in the past. Pray for direction, and you will be guided in your course."

You will be a better person for having done this. Now, if you vote for someone else, my respect for you, as well as my respect for your opinions and choices, will not diminish. The process you personally go through is as important as who you vote for.

I believe a dark horse candidate is needed now more than ever before. As Abraham Lincoln said, "I will prepare myself and my time will come." My fellow Americans, I have prepared myself, and my time has come. I have spent my life settling disputes, resolving problems, facing down bullies, and serving in a number of arenas, including business, politics, education, family and religion. I pledge my allegiance to the Constitution. I am dedicated to correct principles, and I am devoted to God, family and country.

In reality, I desire to be the candidate bringing enlightenment and hope in the upcoming election. The title "Light Horse Candidate" could also be the title of this book. I will bring an enlightened perspective to current issues and concerns. I will give light and meaning in the surrounding darkness of contention and confusion. We can confidently trust in God and recognize His divine purpose and plan to bless our lives and our nation.

Chapter 1

Heritage

In this chapter, I offer a glimpse of my history and heritage so those who may have deeper inquires about me will have a place to start—a jumping-off point—if you will.

My heritage is one of the personal traits that I am delighted to reveal to my fellow Americans. While know more about their favorite movie stars, sports heroes, and music idols than they know about their own grandmother or great-grandfather. We have an obsession with pastimes and leisure. Sadly, one generation works hard and achieves success, only to see the beneficiaries of that success focus their energies on frivolities. When such pastimes eclipse our sense of self and heritage, it's an indicator that society is following the same path of decline as did ancient Rome, Greece and Egypt. Modern examples of nations tell the same story because they took a similar path.

Some may feel justified in their ignorance of heritage, believing their ancestors had inferior technologies and, by association, inferior worldviews. To those who truly believe this, I would urge them to study history more carefully and reconsider such conclusions. I believe labeling former generations as racist, biased, ignorant, or unenlightened would be a serious misjudgment of their character. Certainly there were some people in this nation's history trapped in the bonds of ignorance and vice, but overall their mutual respect, manners, and integrity were in so many ways superior to ours today. I've observed that some people place more emphasis on political correctness and popular worldviews while sadly neglecting the virtues of respect for parents and elders, morality, honesty, personal integrity, and individual responsibility.

Some children may seem justified in rejecting or ignoring their heritage. Perhaps they were genuinely mistreated or neglected by parents and other guardians. Nevertheless, they too can acknowledge that they share a grand heritage indeed.

Today's Americans are the latest in a long line of men and women who came to this country seeking to breathe the fresh and unpolluted air of freedom. Many came to abandon their restrictive, stagnant, and often oppressive countries of origin in search of a new life, a fresh start, and the promise of the fulfillment of grand dreams in a land of opportunity. Many *found* such opportunities and flourished beyond their wildest expectations. They utilized tools that are only available through the freedom and innovation made possible in America.

In other words, most Americans are a direct product of, or are themselves, men and women of dauntless courage, willing to turn their backs on everything they knew in order to reach for something better. In many cases, they abandoned family and possessions in pursuit of a dream, a vision, and conviction that there was something better – liberty.

It was and is this spirit of commitment and adventure—a refusal to give up even in the most challenging of circumstances—that burned in the hearts of our ancestors and in the hearts of many immigrants today. Our pioneer heritage is unparalleled in the history of the world.

We are all a product of that heritage.

HONORING MY ANCESTORS

My great-great-grandfather, Niels Christensen, was a descendent of mighty Viking warriors, explorers and colonizers. As a result of many circumstances influenced by economic and political events, he found himself a humble farmer near Randers, Denmark. He fell in love and married Kristina Marie Nielsen. There were born to them four healthy children—three sons and one daughter—but Kristina's health was questionable.

Their lives and future were dramatically changed when missionaries from America introduced them to a new religion they called the "Restored Gospel" of The Church of Jesus Christ of Latter-day Saints. Niels and the children were baptized and encouraged to gather in "the promised land of Zion" in the United States. It is uncertain whether Kristina did not convert to the LDS Church, didn't want to go, or for some reason was not able to make the journey. In any event, the children were allowed to make their own decisions whether to remain or leave. All chose to leave Denmark with their father and make a new life in America. Kristina stayed behind and was cared for by her parents.

The heart-wrenching experience of saying goodbye to their loving mother, whom they might never see again, was almost too much for the children to bear. This tragic scene remained in their memories for the rest of their lives. Only an overpowering determination enabled them to face westward and begin their long and dangerous journey.

THE PIONEERS

Niels and his son, Niels Christian (my great-grandfather), and the other children, ranging in ages from nine to fifteen, made the arduous journey to America in 1860. They were new converts of a new religion, and came to this country because of the promise of religious freedom. In 1860 this could be a particularly dangerous undertaking for a father with children. Passengers traveling to America from European ports were often instructed to be very careful, to keep their eyes on their luggage *and* on their children. Luggage and private property was often pilfered and stolen. Even more harrowing, children faced the threat of being abducted and sold as slaves.

It's an oft-overlooked fact in history that government-sponsored white slavery flourished in many parts of the world, including in the United States. The practice continued into the nineteenth century, and even later in places like Russia, Asia, and the Middle East (many contend it still takes place today).

By slavery, I don't mean indentured servants who agreed by contract to work for four-to-seven years in order to gain passage to the New World. Slavery was a different thing altogether, and white slaves were generally treated with the same cruelty and indecency as black slaves. Many were transported in the dank, stinking hulls of ships in conditions of such depredation that up to 20 percent died before reaching their destination. They endured chains, malnutrition, beatings, whipping, torture, and remaining in servitude for the rest of their lives.

This report does not remove the awful scar on American history represented by the practice of transporting black slaves. The word "kidnapped" actually originated from the white slave trade. White slaves were often children abducted from innocent families in European and Slavic countries. In the sixteenth century alone, hundreds of thousands of Irish slaves were shipped to America to serve in the booming tobacco industry in Jamestown and in the Caribbean. And even as late as 1860 in European port cities slave traders lurked and preyed upon unsuspecting families of every race.

This fear was recorded in the journals of my ancestors. One emigrant recalled, "I remember how frightened I was when a lady came to my mother to help carry her baby." Her mother, however, judged that something was amiss, and without saying a word, she shook her head, held on tightly to her baby, and walked on.

Passage to America cost approximately $3,000 in gold, an amount that often represented a lifetime of savings. Conditions on the sailing vessels procured by Niels Christensen and his children were unimaginably difficult, even for that day. On May 2, 1860, they sailed from Copenhagen on the steamship *Pauline* to Grimsby, England. Four days later they transferred to a three-decker ship named the *William Tapscott* and set sail from Liverpool for New York Harbor.

 Like most trans-Atlantic voyages, there was much sickness, misery and death among the emigrants. After seventeen days at sea, Maren Christiansen, age thirty-five, who was traveling with Niels and his family, succumbed to the relentless upheaval of the sea. Since sailing fromLiverpool, Maren had been so ill and nauseated that she couldn't keep down any food. On the 17th of May, malnutrition claimed her life. She was buried at sea three and a half hours after her death, leaving her husband alone with their five children. On May 10, Jens, still mourning the loss of his wife less than two weeks earlier, also lost his little one-year-old, Elsie Marie.

Seasickness was a common condition among many of these emigrants, so unaccustomed to ocean voyages. One emigrant tried to help readers envision the awful scene of continuous retching and vomiting: "Such a worshipping of buckets and tins, and unmentionable pans, I shall not attempt to describe. For my part, I paid the most devoted attention to the slop-pail about every half hour." With little or no ventilation, the air was soon permeated with the stench of vomit.

Another passenger, who was experienced at sailing, writes of the effect the North Sea had on his fellow passengers:

> *"What a rotten mess I beheld . . . I did not think that any mortals could live in so much filth. . . . Everybody had vomited over everything; they would vomit and then lay right down in it and never so much as flinch . . . One would think that the angel of death had executed her spell upon them all. Here they lay, big strong men and women, prostrated, just twenty-four hours before full of life and vim singing, 'Farewell, the land of my birth', at the top of their voices, and now they reminded you of a [catch] of dead fish in a net. They were laying over and under each other [and you] could hardly tell who was who. They were indeed more dead than alive. And what a terrible stench! The odor was enough to knock one over and there was no fresh air to be had at all."*

Seasickness was not the only problem that afflicted these passengers. Another was the simple task of cooking their food. *"Cooking for [hundreds of] hungry people at one galley is not a trifling affair."* wrote a passenger of another ship in 1856, *"especially when each family or person has a private pot or dish. Too many pots or dishes at the fire seems as bad as too many irons in it."* Still another passenger referred to the galley as *"the seat of war"* where some would *"fight with bones, kettles, and pans."* Implementing a strict schedule for cooking food was the only thing that maintained any sense of order.

Cleanliness was also a perpetual problem because of the limited supply of fresh water. To hinder the spread of sickness and disease, passengers were strongly urged to keep themselves and their berths clean. This was easier said than done. Fresh water had to be reserved exclusively for drinking and cooking. Passengers were forced to wash themselves and their clothes using salt water on the open deck. Water closets were crude and the rough seas sometimes made using these water closets or toilets a very difficult experience. One young passenger recorded:

> *"The only place I was frightened was when we had to go to the water closet. There was just a straight stick across, and of course you could see the ocean. How I did cling to my little sister when she was on that bar, for it was big enough to let a grown person down, let alone children."*

Monotony, boredom, and cramped quarters also took their toll. The travelers, however, did what they could to pass the time with a positive attitude: visiting, holding meetings, making new acquaintances, reading, scanning the horizon, and dreaming of life in America. During the voyage from Liverpool, England, there were ten deaths among the passengers, four babies born, and nine couples married.

The eastern tip of Long Island was sighted on June 14. The following day, the ship docked in the New York harbor, over a month after its initial departure. Because smallpox had broken out on the ship, all passengers were vaccinated, and the ship was held in quarantine for five days. Some of the ill were taken to Staten Island. Several of those who had died were buried on that island.

By recounting these details, I don't mean to highlight the experiences of my ancestors as peculiar or unique. These were the common hardships experienced by many emigrants. These men and women were heartily willing to endure any level of discomfort, carried forward by the hopes of a better life in a "promised land." From their written accounts it is very clear that their dreams of life in America—of becoming *Americans*—was so overpowering that trying to prevent or delay their journey would have been like trying to stop the forces of a hurricane with an umbrella. Except for today's immigrants who still yearn to come to the United States, few today can appreciate the drive and determination—the hope for a better life—that guided these pioneers. Too few remember, or have ever even been taught, the incredible sacrifices of our immigrant ancestors.

I am grateful that my ancestral heritage has been an integral part of my life from my earliest years and burns inside me like a bonfire. My main goal to serve as a "statesman president" is to reignite that same appreciation—that brand of patriotism—in the minds of hearts of all Americans. Why? Because one thing is certain: the freedoms our forebears fought for—the freedoms they gained so we could experience the prosperity we enjoy today—can be lost far more easily than you can imagine. It is my purpose to reawaken and reignite that passion in your soul. It is only in and through understanding and gratitude that we can save and preserve the United States that I have known and treasured throughout my life.

After my great-great-grandfather, Niels Christensen, arrived in New York, he and his young children traveled up the Hudson River by steamship to Albany, New York. Their company of primarily Scandinavians soon left Albany and traveled by train to Rochester and then on to Niagara Falls, and from Windsor to Detroit, from Chicago to Quincy, Illinois, and finally to St. Joseph, Missouri. From St. Joseph they went by flat boat up the Missouri River to Florence, Nebraska, arriving on July 4, 1860.

Niels Christensen and his children were only one family among the 80,000 immigrant members of The Church of Jesus Christ of Latter-day Saints to settle in America. Some of these pioneers rode in wagons; others with dogged determination pulled all their earthly possessions across the plains in handcarts—shallow wagons with two large wheels and a bar that extended at the front of the wagon that was pulled by one or two people standing side-by-side, clutching the bar and walking. Many just walked. More than 6,000 of these pioneers died along the way. Their purpose? To worship their God according to the dictates of their conscience, and to allow all men the same privilege.

In Nebraska, Niels Christensen, and family along with 400 Scandinavian, Swiss, South African and British men and women took only two weeks to get ready for a thousand-mile trek to the Great Salt Lake Valley of the Utah Territory. They left Florence on July 19, 1860, with 55 wagons, 215 oxen and 77 cows. This was the last wagon train company for that season and one of the largest to cross the plains. Niels had secured one wagon, four oxen and three cows. Their wagon train experienced many of the challenges met by others. There was heat, rain, river crossings, wolves, Indians, births, deaths, and exhausting work. Neils Christian wrote, "During the last three nights we had scarcely had any sleep owing to the annoyance of mosquitoes." He also said that a "fearful storm made travel very unpleasant. The downfall was so plentiful that we could scarcely move because of the water."

At one point in the journey there were 1500 to 2000 Indians, including men, women and children, surrounding the wagon train. The Indian tribe had many dogs and horses who traveled with them. Niels also wrote, "We were very much amused to witness their peculiar mode of travel, with their long tent poles and other equipment." One night after a Scandinavian man died, his wife wept bitterly for his loss. Her sorrow brought Indians to comfort her and cry on her shoulder. Her son later wrote, "It was wonderful to see the sympathy and pity and weeping for mother by those large husky women of the Great Sioux Nation, out in the wilderness on the Plains of Wyoming." For the next few weeks, the Indians camped very close to the immigrants. Niels Christian continued:

"We resumed our journey at 5:45 a.m. The whole body of Indians traveled with us, or went in the same direction that we were going, but we had to stop while they passed us. They made us understand that they were going into war with another tribe which had killed some of their women and children while the men were out to hunt. After the Indians had encamped a short distance ahead of us, a number of them came back to our camp in the evening begging for something to eat."

While the Indians journeyed alongside them, the immigrants killed several cows to help feed their native traveling companions. In return, the Indians gave them wild cherries.

The wagon company arrived in Salt Lake City on October 5, 1860. The journey had taken almost three months. Eventually, Niels Christensen took his family north to the stunningly beautiful Cache Valley and settled in what is now Hyrum, Utah. Niels and the family all wept when they received news from Denmark that their beloved wife and mother, Kristine, had died. Later, Niels married Karen Sorenson and had eleven more children.

My great-grandfather, Niels Christian, like his father became a man of great faith, devoted to perpetual service in his church and community. Having known the hardships of his parents during his youth, he was always grateful for his situation in life and felt he had plenty to suit his own needs and a consistent surplus to share with needy widows and others in the community. No government program was necessary to teach him these values. These were the guiding principles of his life. His family described him as somebody who never sought personal recognition or praise for his service. He was a quiet, humble man, considerate and aware of the needs of those around him, and a hard worker who spent long hours on the farm. He worked not only his own crops, but he was always available to help other farmers who needed help. His life span was only sixty-one years. In his 62nd year he underwent operation for a hernia at home, and did not survive the anesthesia. His death was an enormous shock to his family who had never known him to be anything but fit, active, and hard-working, even up to a few days before his passing.

THE BUILDERS

My grandfather, Christian H. Christensen, was the oldest of eleven children. After his father's death, Christian devoted his energies to helping his family and married when he was twenty-six years old. He had fallen in love with the tall and slender Bena Marie Frogner, of Swedish and Norwegian ancestry, whom he had known all his life.

Christian served as the constable for the city of Logan, Utah, in his younger days. He was described as having "the longest reach and hardest punch of any man in Logan." Apparently this was the trait that qualified him for the job. At six feet in height and weighing 180 pounds he was known to the community as "Big Chris". Evidently in those days a dance or party wasn't a *real* dance or party unless you had a rollicking brawl. Such events frequently required the stern intervention of my grandfather.

Christian and Bena moved to Idaho in the spring of 1897 with a son who was barely a year old. They transported all of their belongings, which included a team and wagon, a cow, chickens, bed and bedding, dresser, cupboard, stove, a bin for flour, hay and grain for the animals, a few potatoes, water and what other food and clothing could fit into the wagon. It took them almost a month to reach their destination in Goshen, Idaho.

Bena's hearing was impaired from scarlet fever as a child. Nevertheless, her journals tell of her enduring faith in God and her unique gifts to "hear the voice of the Lord." On one occasion a bloated cow that had eaten too much green alfalfa came up to the house and lay across the doorway in an obvious state of misery. My grandmother knew if she didn't act quickly the cow would not survive. This would have had a devastating impact upon her family. She happened to have her sewing scissors in hand and felt a strong impression of how to rectify the situation. She leaned over the cow and stabbed the scissors into the animal's bloated side. A fountain of sloppy green hay and gas spewed as high as the roof. When the gas and grass stopped shooting out, the cow got back to her feet and wandered away to live for many more years.

Another recorded event involved my grandmother's younger son, my Uncle Matt, who was on his way home in the old family car. Grandma was working in her kitchen when she felt impressed to walk down the road along the canal. She felt an inner sense that something was desperately wrong and her son was in grave danger. She found the car overturned in the canal, with Matt trapped inside. My grandmother played an indispensable part in saving his life.

My maternal grandmother, Esther Swift, was born in Barnsley, Yorkshire, England, on December 22, 1885. She married my grandfather, William Thornton, in December, 1905. William had been raised a Quaker, working in the coal mines of Yorkshire from the time he was twelve years old. As a young man, William began attending the Methodist Church and preached the ways of the Methodists on the streets of his town. One day a friend invited him to get acquainted with the "Brighamites," which was their way of describing two Mormon Latter-day Saint elders (named after the second leader of the LDS Church, Brigham Young). During the meeting, my grandfather was deeply moved by the missionaries' message.

During the course of the discussion, however, the friend who had invited him to attend became angry and left. When William's father found out that he was "going around" with the LDS missionaries, William was warned to "leave home or leave them Mormons alone." William not only left home, but eventually left his native land and moved to America with Esther and their baby daughter, Elsie. Their ship eventually docked in Montreal, Canada. His young family worked their way across the country, finally settling in Coleville, Utah, where their second daughter, Marvilla, was born. Eighteen months later, my mother, Esther, was born.

As with many births in those days, it was a difficult delivery, with multiple complications for the mother. The doctor told William that his wife was going to die. However, it was attributed to the power of faith that both survived, and my grandmother lived to give birth to five more children.

William served many missions for the LDS Church, which in those days required an extraordinary sacrifice of finances and up to three years of time. Once, while serving away from home, one of his bottom teeth came loose. He pulled it out, scraped it with his pocket knife, and pressed it back into place in his gums. Afterward he got down on knees and prayed "that my tooth might stay as tight as any of the others in my mouth." Apparently this act of faith worked, as the tooth remained in place for many years thereafter. I found an interesting passage in his journal, where he noted that "one must keep this type of experience to oneself as it is hard for people to believe these things." His journals tell of other experiences that he and his descendants consider very sacred.

On William's second mission, he was assigned to the Central States Mission headquartered in Independence, Missouri. He had full confidence that the Lord would look after his family in his absence. He enjoyed his forty-fifth birthday on the same day his companion turned the ripe old age of nineteen. During grandfather's lifetime he served a total of eight missions, including two to his native England. On his last mission, he had the privilege of serving with his wife, Esther, shortly after the close of the World War II.

HONORING MY PARENTS

My father, Irven Christensen, was born in a log cabin in Goshen, Bingham County, Idaho, on June 21, 1899. My mother, Esther Thornton, was born in Evanston, Wyoming, in 1911 and was my father's second wife. His first wife had died. Irven lived and worked as hard as did his parents and grandparents before him. During his ninety years, he witnessed the advent of automobiles, airplanes and rocket ships transporting men to the moon. He witnessed many scientific, medical, and other technological advances. He also lived through World War I, the Great Depression, World War II, the Korean and Vietnam Wars, and the Cold War with the Soviet Union. He often told me how he personally observed a change in American values, and how the virtues of hard work were replaced by leisure and entertainment. He was an optimist, but he was also very concerned that character, nobility, and beauty were steadily overshadowed by vice, crime and pornography. It was his opinion that the twentieth century were the best of years and the worst of years for the United States.

Because of my father's sense of responsibility to provide for the needs of his siblings, he went to work and never received his high school degree. In 1920, he married Lucy Irene Davis, with whom he had five children. With a growing family, he returned to complete his high school education, earned his college degree, and even pursued graduate work. He worked in numerous capacities in many small-town and country schools, serving as an administrator and teacher of science, math and other subjects. My father loved to read and study everything in preparation for what he called his "final exam" when he would stand before God to be judged for his life on earth. This exam began for him when he passed away in October, 1990.

My father had a very pleasant manner in his associations with everyone he met. I will always remember how much he loved people in general and how they loved him. More than any other attribute, I hope this is the one that I have inherited from him. Another attribute I hope I inherited was his talent as a peacemaker. People often came to our home to receive his counsel and find comfort. I suppose his true gift was that he was a great listener. This trait naturally made people feel he truly understood and empathized with their problems. I recall that one of the most common pieces of advice he gave was to seek out and help someone else who had a problem greater than theirs. When the people he talked with did this, they frequently found that their own problems were diminished or went away entirely.

After twenty years of marriage, when my sisters Gene was a teenager and Theda Lou was twelve, Lucy fell ill with a kidney disorder and was taken to the hospital in an ambulance. She required a blood transfusion, but she didn't survive long enough to receive it. Dad was sitting in the waiting room when the doctor came out and apologized by saying, "There was nothing we could do for her."

After Lucy's death, my father remained single for a time until he was finally introduced to my mother, Esther Thornton, by my oldest sister. My parents married in 1942 and had five more children. A year after my birth in 1948, my father moved our family to Blackfoot, Idaho, where he lived until he died. I have never met a person more at peace with himself or as genuinely happy as my father.

Dad tried to retire many times over the course of his life, but never could embrace the concept of not working. Even into his eighties he was engaged in building, renovation, farming, gardening, and other labors that men in their twenties would find difficult to perform. The eternal theme he would recite to his children was, "Remember who you are and act accordingly," by which he meant to honor our heritage and live in a way that would make God and our ancestors proud. He would also say to departing guests, "Tell your folks what we think of them". And "Would you rather live in the country or in the summer"?

My mother, Esther, attended LDS Business College and was their oldest alumni when she passed away in 2008 at ninety-seven years of age. Mother made the best of trying to be a second mother to my older siblings and living in Idaho, away from the rest of her family. Mother was always cheerful, yearned to please, and had a gentle and angelic spirit. She was always sensitive to the needs of others, so much so that her constant worrying resulted in her having a debilitating stomach ulcer. In the late 1950s, she had a large portion of her stomach removed and could only eat small meals for the rest of her life. Nevertheless, she always exercised, ate well, and got the proper amount of rest. She memorized many long poems, stories, and had a sense of humor that she never tired of sharing. She was proud of her role as a full-time mother and homemaker, preparing delicious homemade meals, kissing everyone good-bye, and welcoming them home with a big hug.

Mom never lacked for things to keep her busy. Dad would often gently chide her by saying, "That can wait until next August," or "Hurry up and wait." She just went on cooking, sewing, canning fruits and vegetables, cleaning house, doing laundry, washing dishes, etc. Even when Dad and the children helped, she would simply go on and do other chores. She loved to read and was determined to learn the Spanish language even into her eighties and early nineties. If my mother had any fault I believe it was that she worked harder than she should have and worried far too much. But this was her nature, and there wasn't a thing that anyone could have done to change it.

If any single person is responsible for developing my self-esteem, it would be my mother. From the time I was only four or five years old she would tell others that I was a great help to her in the kitchen because I would assist her in the important tasks of baking cakes and cooking other dishes. This made me feel very big and important. I was determined to help her do the laundry in the days when we had a big gray washing machine with ringers. She was always concerned that I might get my fingers caught in the ringers, so she would patiently guide my hands during the process. She laughed when I did funny things, praised me when I was good, and wept when she had to discipline me. Her work ethic was contagious. We all learned to work. My mother told me I could do anything. I put my mind to, including someday becoming the President of the United States. I believed her.

Mother personally insured that we always had a Christmas tree and memorable holidays, birthdays, and other special occasions. She took us fishing and packed picnics when we went to hunt asparagus along the ditch banks. She always had clean, pressed clothes for me to wear to school. I loved their smell and the smell of my clean sheets when I went to bed. My family was not rich by any means, but my mother made do with what she had, and whatever she had was always transformed into something better.

Despite her work ethic, she was always ready to go someplace and to have fun. In her old age, with arthritis in her fingers, she started to practice on the piano. Her mind was always clear and her heart pure. She had no fear of death, only of hurting someone's feelings. After my father died, she longed to be with him, as well as with her deceased parents and other family. She loved to eat Chinese food and converse with my aunts— her sisters—all talking at the same time and telling each other the same familiar jokes. I used to wonder if maybe it was the Chinese food!

Mother had a firm conviction of Jesus Christ and his Gospel that welled up so strong that from a very young age I knew *she* knew. Because of her strength I could not doubt such knowledge. She radiated love, goodness, and a child-like, Christ-like sweetness towards everyone, including the poor and the unpopular. Mother was a holy person.

OVERRIDING THEMES

We are all a product of those who came before us. The reason I recount with such passion and endearment the details of my heritage is certainly not to boast, but to share a heritage we all have. My heritage is yours and yours is mine. I am grateful for my ancestors. I realize my story is more the rule than the exception when it comes to spotlighting the quality of those citizens who built this nation. Moreover, we are *all* the products of our heritage. Certainly there are many examples of individuals who came from horrible circumstances, and perhaps even parents and grandparents of questionable character, but who then rose above the expectations generally associated with such origins to become outstanding contributors to society— in *spite* of their family tree.

Most Americans are the product of pioneers, dreamers, innovators, and visionary leaders who were the cream of the societies from which they emigrated. They may have been hungry and poor, but they were and are the best of the best, and they came to this country because their gifts and talents could not flourish in their native lands or governments.

Some may find the frequent themes of faith and religion in my narrative to be offensive. It's best to get used to it now because I can assure my readers that such themes will persist throughout this book. My conviction is that those in this country who are offended by religious devotion are an outspoken minority of citizens. While I treasure the freedoms that enable them to make a stand for their beliefs and positions, I will not shrink from representing my own sentiments. It's time that Americans of all faiths stood tall and acknowledged that most Americans are the direct *products* of such faith and religious devotion. The journals and histories of my ancestors are *rife* with religion, *teeming* with spiritual experiences, and born of a conviction that blessings are imparted from a Higher Source. If I sought to minimize that reality in any way, it would not only be a denial of my heritage, it would be a denial of my very being and who I am.

Chapter 2

"H"

SHAPING MY IDENTITY

Now that my ancestors have been introduced, I'd like to introduce myself in a more formal manner. My full name is Dale H Christensen. Some may have noticed there is no period after my middle initial. This is not a typo. My middle name really is just an "H" without a period. The H was given to me as a middle initial in honor of my grandfather, Christian H. Christensen. In my grandfather's case, putting a period after his middle initial seems consistent in family records, but no one seems to recall what the H actually stood for. Some suspect it may have been Henry since he gave that name to one of his sons, but this theory hasn't been verified. It's a minor family mystery which I inherited.

Beyond this, my family was very consistent and diligent about keeping journals and histories. Even I am often stunned by the frankness of my ancestor's records, honestly depicting both the positive and negative traits and events that shaped their lives. I feel honored to have been able to reflect on those examples of integrity and hard work in my own life, striving to build on their success and avoid many of their mistakes.

I was born on July 5, 1948 in Shelley, Bingham County, Idaho, as the eighth of ten children—four brothers and five sisters. In our modern age, the concept of a family having so many children is sometimes perceived as irresponsible and supported by a scarcity mentality. Financial opportunity is too often valued over a moral foundation and a firm commitment to the principals of self-reliance. Some expect to have things handed to them on a silver platter. They often resent their parents when they "fail" to supply their wants. Parents naturally want to bless their children, but no one wants an attitude of entitlement and lack of gratitude.

I invite anyone to recognized personal flaws to join with others to work together and turn the tide away from self-indulgence toward self-sufficiency. We can improve the economy; make education and health benefits more affordable, while instilling cherished values that include performance and reward. Coming from a big family taught me how to work, contribute, share, sacrifice, be self-reliant and responsible, not to expect things or to be entitled etc.

My father was a humble man who always provided for his family, but placed far more emphasis upon instilling virtue, values and example in the hearts and minds of his children and others rather than a dependence upon money. He strived to help me understand my relationship to God and man, to set my priorities in order, and to analyze, evaluate with adequate foresight, and finally to prayerfully look to a Higher Source to aid in problem solving. He blessed me with adequate health, mental stability, and wisdom to make sensible decisions. I learned to set and achieve short and long-range goals for my personal good as well as for the good of my family. As a boy, I knew I had an important work to do. I had no fear of hard manual labor and sincerely wanted to be out with the men hoeing beets, driving trucks, bucking hay, harvesting spuds, etc. I was so ambitious and enthusiastic that my parents always cautioned me to look ahead, slow down, and be careful. I still have this enthusiasm for a meaningful life today.

While I maintain this zest for life and progress, I believe I can also provide America with the desperately needed wisdom and a spirit of discernment to lead the United States at this most critical time.

EARLY LESSONS AND OBSERVATIONS

World War II ended just prior to my birth. The Korean conflict took place when I was a boy. The Cold War with Russia and China and its fears of nuclear annihilation seemed to ever be in a state of escalation. Even so, my family always prayed for the starving and needy families and children in those countries. When I was sixteen years old, President John F. Kennedy was assassinated. Like every other American of that generation, I remember exactly where I was and what I was doing when I heard the news. I was walking through the cafeteria in the basement of Blackfoot High School. Shortly thereafter, the Civil Rights movement and the Vietnam War were causes of great unrest in our nation. At the same time, the influences of immorality and drug use were growing across America and in my own small community.

Because of the Space Race and a healthy and active competition between nations, NASA was able to put a man on the moon and launch countless satellites into orbit. The world witnessed miraculous scientific discoveries that have catapulted our communication technologies forward, with thousands of television channels and billions of websites, social network connections, and mobile technologies. The Worldwide Web has saturated our daily lives with all forms of entertainment. There have been many pharmaceutical and chemical breakthroughs. Nevertheless, the world is also increasingly dependent upon medicine, cosmetics, and chemicals. Many of the common-sense approaches and solutions to life that were utilized and implemented routinely by my parents' generation have fallen by the wayside. New products developed from petroleum have made this substance one of the most valuable commodities across the globe. Oil has become the spark for contention in many parts of the world, particularly in the Middle East, culminating in such conflicts as the Gulf War and wars in Iraq and Afghanistan.

On the domestic front and worldwide, the family is being eroded through many indirect means, and is under very deliberate attack by others through methods both subtle and overt. A dramatic change in food consumption and eating habits has rapidly destroyed the traditional family mealtime. Parents and children no longer bond at the dinner table and discuss the events and challenges of their day. We have become a society in which fast foods and frozen prepared meals have isolated family members from one another. Meals are quickly eaten on the run or consumed while sitting in front of televisions and computers.

Divorce has become an accepted and easy process and has replaced the concepts of persevering, forgiving, recommitment, and working out problems together. During my lifetime I've watched the United States evolve from a nation where abortion was unthinkable or extremely rare into a nation where millions of unborn children have been denied life. Some ethnic groups in the United States are actually now experiencing a negative growth rate in their overall population.

Moreover, I've witnessed our society change from one in which a mother was revered and supported in her choice to be a mother and homemaker to a society where she may be ostracized or belittled for that decision. The American economy and a perceived need for a certain level of prosperity have demanded that a family must have two wage earners to make ends meet.

Domestic violence is on the rise. Its effects are being seen on the streets and in the classrooms. Some children are becoming more disrespectful of their parents and teachers. They make bold displays of vulgarity without conscience.

Many artists, actors, and musicians have created masterpieces that have inspired the human spirit, while others in those same creative fields have produced an assortment of profane and degrading works that are destructive to the human soul. A general spirit of contention, rebellion, and discontent are entering our hearts, flowing into our streets, and spreading like a plague through our cities and towns. During all of this, the square footage of our homes has been increasing. Automobiles have gotten bigger and faster. Many people have become wealthier, while others have fallen onto hard times. Some entirely abandon their religious faith in favor of secular science.

Technologies have developed to increase our access to information in ways that our predecessors could not have imagined. This has provided unprecedented opportunities to become more educated and industrious. At the same time, such technologies have been used to promote pornography, violence, bullying, and crime. Social media was introduced to bring people together and allow them to correspond at the speed of light. At the same time it is consuming the lives of too many who find themselves unable to participate in normal, healthy human associations. Technology has improved people's standard of living, allowing them to accomplish far more in a shorter period of time through instant messaging, e-mail, and conference calling. Ironically, it's been my personal observation that the general quality of people's lives, their inner sense of happiness and fulfillment, as well as their self-esteem, has experienced a precipitous decline.

Undoubtedly some will judge my observations as out-of-touch, naive, and a solid evidence of the generation gap that exists between the modern age and old fuddy-duddies of a bygone generation. However, I'm convinced that most will perceive a spirit of truth in my observations and experience a feeling of commonality with my life experiences. Despite my observations, I remain fundamentally optimistic about the future and our potential to recapture the values that made America a powerhouse of good in the world. It will take work, it will take dedication, and it will take a fresh dynamic of mutual cooperation between factions now at odds with one another. But that's the movement I want to lead, and that's the reason I'm running for President.

My mother was visionary when she informed me that I could one day run for President of the United States. But at the time, these aspirations were far from my mind. My favorite pastime was traveling with my father to the Blackfoot Indian Reservation. He had work to do for the coming school year. While he talked to the parents I ran and played with my Native American friends and didn't want to go home when the time came.

These Native Americans lived in very humble circumstances, but so did I. My bedroom with my brother was on the closed-in back porch of our home. It had windows, but was freezing in the winter and sweltering in the summer. On cold winter nights, snow blew in under the back door and drifted up around the buckets filled with coal that we'd hauled from the coal shed by the back alley. During summer nights the setting sun heated up the back porch, so we opened the windows and door to let in fresh air. We could never keep the mosquitoes out.

Because I was tall for my age, many of the older boys picked fights with me. I learned very young to stand my ground and fight my hardest even if I was taking a beating. A good thing happened when a boy three years older and almost a foot taller than me wanted to fight outside the public swimming pool. It had just closed, but the grassy yard was somewhat illuminated by the ball field lights across the street. After several attempts to walk away, I threw my towel and swimming suit on the ground and squared off with my challenger. When he came at me, I gave him everything I had and knocked him back on the ground. He got up two more times and I laid him out twice more. With a bloody nose and wounded pride, he offered his hand, and I never had that problem again.

A few years later, the same thing happened in nearby Idaho Falls when I was visiting relatives. Another bully started to pick on me because I couldn't stand up on skates. I took them off and fought him in my stocking feet. He went running home with a bloody nose to get his big brother, who was an even bigger bully. Dick, Ray and I ran home down the bottom of the dry canal to stay out of sight.

DREAMS OF JOHNNY UNITAS

Johnny Unitas was one of my childhood heroes, and you can see why when you read this:

> *"Notre Dame thought Johnny Unitas was too small. The Pittsburgh Steelers thought he wasn't smart enough. The Baltimore Colts got it right. Unitas, 6-feet and 145 pounds in high school, became a nowhere-to-somewhere story, a backup who kept getting opportunities to succeed at every level. 'Give me a chance,' the crew-cut quarterback would say, 'and I'll show you.' He went from semi-pro dirt fields to stardom with the Colts in the National Football League. And he did it quickly. 'The most important thing of all about Unitas,' said Weeb Ewbank, his Colts coach, 'is that he had a real hunger. This was a kid who wanted success and didn't have it so long that he wasn't about to waste it when it came.'"*
>
> - Bob Carter, interview to ESPN, *Unitas Surprised Them All*

If there's one overriding description of my interests as a young man, it was my love of sports. My father often resorted to sports analogies and metaphors to make his points. A family Christmas letter from 1960 described me in one of its paragraphs:

"Dale (now 12) feeds us athletics for breakfast, dinner and supper. We never know whether he is going to throw us for a loss behind the line of scrimmage or go out of the game (either in the living room or kitchen) for personal fouls. Has been in little league baseball for three years now and started scouting . . ."

Our 1962 family Christmas letter said:

"Then there's the Freshman, DALE, who likes to do almost anything as long as it is baseball, football, basketball or any other kind of ball playing. He manages to get grades that will permit him to be on all the teams. He has really grown up physically in the last year. I dare say, he's grown up in other respects also. It is a question as to whether his good looks are just his Mother's opinion or whether he actually is as handsome as his doctor said he was at six-weeks-of-age. Anyway, he has quite a sense of humor. And he loves to tease."

Others have reminded me that when I was a boy I was full of energy and mischief. I pulled girls' hair, hit other boys, and got into more than my share of trouble. I know I was sometimes happy, but there were many times I felt the keen emotions of sadness and anger. My fifth-grade teacher, Mrs. Hill, went out of her way to make me feel much better about myself. Like so many other wonderful and inspired teachers, she was a stellar example of someone who performed her job with passion and a burning desire to make a difference. It was my special privilege at this tender age that she took a special interest in me and assigned me various chores and other responsibilities. This wasn't work to me. It was an honor to be so selected. I began to love her, and to this day I am grateful for what she did for me.

My older brothers and sisters (Lea, Lynn, Gene, Theda Lou and Myrol) were my heroes and second parents. My siblings closer to my age (Art, Dian, Kay and Karl) were my guardians and guideposts. They all married wonderful people and had exceptional families. Because my older siblings were so much older than me, I grew up with my nieces and nephews as though they were my cousins. My dear friends (Lenny Ralphs, Ken Henderson, Mark Beebe, Pat Hoge, Sharon Gardner, Katie Farnes, etc.) influenced me for good and helped me to do my best and make good choices. They helped me feel I had greatness inside of me. They gave me a desire to be discovered in a big way.

I considered myself a fairly devout and dedicated student. I loved the sciences and took particular pleasure in the subjects of physiology and zoology. I kept all of my science papers from this time period, but preserved only a few excerpts from some of my English papers about work, thinking, and family. I must confess that I struggled in English. My high school English teacher, Mrs. Owens, was very disappointed in me because my older brother and sister had been among her best pupils. During the second week of class, she said in front of all the other students, "Dale Christensen, what happened to *you!*" Needless to say, I was quite embarrassed and humiliated.

In this same English class a friend of mine, Steve Price, got an A for writing the following character sketch of me:

"Dale is a tall, bushy headed athlete. He is as strong minded as a bull moose. One couldn't get Dale to change his mind even if the world was falling in. He is just that type of guy. Dale will give you the sweat off from his brow; but if you cross him once,

you have lost a close friend for a while, anyway. His dark features and his boney frame are a picture of readiness before a basketball or football game. In his sports he is a dedicated worker who will pay—the—price to play. Even when the sweat is running out of his coal black hair and down his dark face to his square chin, he will not stop working. His light blue eyes have an eerie twinkle when he is mad. His oversized fingers are a sign of friendship when he is happy, but are coiled and ready to strike when he is mad. He has some good points, and some bad ones, yet he is the best friend a person could ever have."

It's no exaggeration that I loved to participate in virtually every sport, especially basketball, football, volleyball, and tennis. I played pretty well, and my teams won a fair share of games, but we never achieved our goal of winning a state championship. There was something about the thrill of the game and the challenge to excel and succeed that made me want to be an outstanding athlete. As I reflect back on outstanding moments of heroism in high school and college sports, I realize that life is much like a sports contest. We must practice and work hard for long periods of time in order to participate and excel in triumph or defeat. Sports were good for me because they taught me excellence, discipline, and teamwork.

Now I'm going to confess to a part of my personality some might feel exposes my deep sentimentality. During my high school years I watched the movies *Mary Poppins* and *The Sound of Music*. These movies had a profound effect upon me. I was transformed. I lost my anger, felt happy, and wanted to do something good in the world. It may sound odd, but after I saw those two movies my life began to be more devoted to worthwhile pursuits and more centered on following the example of my Savior, Jesus Christ. I dedicated my life to serving my fellow human beings. Then my teacher, Jay Todd, recommended that we read the book *Magnificent Obsession* by Lloyd C. Douglas. After completing that book I had a strong desire to share the good that was in the world with everyone I could touch. These seemingly ordinary works of popular art served as an indescribable springboard for my life. I believe they helped steer me in the right direction. I've always had a great respect for artists who seek to build up mankind rather than tear it down. I've tried to reward such efforts throughout my life.

FIRST INTERNATIONAL ADVENTURE

During our summer family reunion in 1965, my older brother, Lynn, and his wife, Ruth, came from England with their family to our home in Blackfoot for a family reunion. My niece, Suzanne, who was a year younger than me, invited me to come and live with them in London and attend London's Central High School for my senior year, which was a school associated with the American Air Force Base at South Ruislip. Most of my fellow students would be American "military brats," as they called themselves, who had moved often and lived in many parts of the world. I didn't know if I wanted to leave my hometown because I'd planned with my teammates to win the state championship in basketball. That all changed when Suzanne informed me that their school in London played all the same American sports with other military base schools across the continent of Europe.

The adventure captured my interest. Lynn, Ruth, and Suzanne somehow managed to convince my parents. At the end of the summer, I was on my way to take advantage of my first international travel experience and living in a foreign country. I was on the adventure of a lifetime, for which I was not very well prepared.

Heading east on the train, I spoke to lots of people and got off to see Chicago and New York before boarding a jet to England by way of Iceland and Scotland. During the three days in the "Big Apple", I got to visit all the sites including the Statue of Liberty, Empire State Building and the World's Fair. It was an amazing experience.

When I landed in Glasgow, the immigration authorities thought I looked like a person who wanted to get into Europe and just live off the land. I couldn't understand them very well, but I could clearly see the concern on their faces about me entering their country. Except for the clothes I had on, everything I owned was in the cardboard box I was carrying. I had no money, couldn't remember the name of the school I was supposed to attend, or the town where I was going to live. I was an immigrant. The officers caused me to miss my connecting flight. They were ready to send me back to New York on the next flight at 2:00 a.m. When my worried family realized I'd missed my flight, they finally got through on the telephone and rescued me.

I know what it's like to be an immigrant. I understand the emotions of coming to a country where you might not be welcomed. I also know that there are effective ways to protect a nation's borders and national security and to enforce immigration laws. My older brother, Lynn, worked for Chicago Bridge and Iron and supervised work across Europe and the Middle East. Ruth soon became my second mother.

My first day on the school bus, there were many students smoking and swearing in the seats behind us and at the back of the bus. They were obviously a bit more experienced in the ways of the world in comparison to a small-town Idaho farm boy. This type of language and behavior disturbed me. It continued for some time until I turned around and raised my voice, "Hey, listen fellas, I'm sitting with my niece. She's a lady and I would appreciate it if you wouldn't talk like that around her."

There was immediate silence and looks of surprise. Some got up and moved to the rear of the bus. Suzanne's face flushed with surprise, but also admiration. I apologized to her for what the guys had said and told her I hoped it hadn't embarrassed her. She said, "No, no, I hear that kind of thing all the time. I just haven't heard anyone tell them to stop. That was so neat. I'm so proud of you!"

I began to love learning and to love people. We had calculus and trigonometry class with Mr. Rutan, government with Mr. Green, and Greek mythology and English literature with Mrs. Threlkheld. Even in England, I managed to enjoy the sports of American football and basketball, as well as the international sport of tennis. All of these sports were directed by Coach Lewis, a man who had the distinction of being a former U.S. Olympian discus and javelin thrower. In Great Britain the past came to life, the present became important, and the future bloomed with possibilities. Without a doubt, it was a marvelous and life-changing year for me.

On the day of football tryouts several players introduced themselves and asked what position I played. Without reservation I said I was a quarterback. Their reply was that they already had a quarterback. Besides, they thought I was too tall for that position. However, during practice the ends and half-backs loved my passing, especially going long. That day, Coach Lewis announced I would be the team quarterback.

FIRST GAME—ORLEANS, FRANCE

The big day finally arrived for our first game on our home field. No one really talked much about winning, just by how many points we were expected to lose. Orleans, France was one of the largest U.S. Army bases in Europe and had a large student body. They'd been a powerhouse the year before. Their starters had all returned, and every one of them was big and brutal. The sports section of the *Stars and Stripes* (*S&S*) had predicted that Orleans would win 18 to 8. Others thought it would be more like 27 to 0.

We played on the South Ruislip Air Force Base football field. The spectators included parents, cheerleaders, a small band, and our loyal student cheering section. There were also some airmen from the base.

The opposing team took the field. And that's just what they seemed to do as they stormed out in their orange and black trimmed uniforms—*take* the field. Our team, the Central High School Bobcats, wearing our humble blue jerseys, seemed dwarfed in comparison by numbers and average size. The Air Force had always prided itself on intelligence and mobility. Historically, the Army dominated the land and the Air Force dominated the skies. On that day, it was questionable if we were going to be able to dominate anything.

THE ROSY RED BOMB

We lost the coin toss and kicked off. Their record from the previous year began to repeat itself as they steadily marched downfield, gaining 6 to 10 yards on each play. We just didn't seem to be a worthy match. Their linemen were so much larger, with many backfield players as tall or even taller than me. Because of our small numbers, most of our players played double-duty on defense and offense. On defense, I played cornerback and safety. With each tackle they were hitting us hard—much harder than we were used to during practices. Every player developed the same forlorn expression that seemed to say, "This is going to be a very long day." We quickly found ourselves defending at our own 30-yard line.

Moments later they were inside our 25 and pulsing with momentum. Suddenly, in a moment of backfield confusion, they fumbled the ball, and our safety, Jeff McComb, recovered on our 21-yard line. He was all of 5-foot 8-inches and 140 pounds, but he was a real fighter.

We were introduced to their defensive team. The Bobcats ran two plays and lost yardage on each attempt. It was obvious that we needed to come up with something creative. In the next huddle, I called the play: "Rosy Red Bomb on 2."

The Rosy Red Bomb was an innovative play intended for special situations. I decided this was just such a situation. The formation during this play was unusual. Both ends and tackles and both half-backs were split wide in preparation for an obvious pass. I lined up on the shotgun position about eight yards behind the center and two offensive guards. Bob Brandt, the fullback, was set to block as I dropped back for the pass. The ends went deep and the half-backs crisscrossed. The tackles were supposed to move laterally to take their man away from the play. If the defensive tackle chose to remain near the ball and rushed the quarterback it was fairly easy to pass laterally to the split halfback. Otherwise, the objective was long yardage—something we needed desperately. I must have felt that anything else seemed useless against this fresh defensive team, who appeared even meaner than their offensive players.

In the huddle, I told my center, "Hamish, make it a good snap." I said to my wide receivers, "Max and Calvin, you guys go deep as fast as you can." I told my fullback, "Bob, you've got to block and give me some time. Everybody ready? Okay, break!"

As our players fanned out on the line of scrimmage, the defensive players were so confused that they called for a man-to-man defense. Curious comments came from the spectators. This gave me hope. I was confident that no one could keep up with our tight end, Calvin Bradley. He was faster than anyone in the league and at 6'1" he could out-jump most basketball players who were six inches taller.

"Ready, down, hut 1, hut 2!"

It was a good snap and my pass receivers were off. So far, the play didn't seem especially difficult to execute. I dropped back, worked my way to the right, and waited as long as I could before I let 'er go with all I had. I'd watched Calvin start to gain ground on the safety guarding him. I spun, trying to avoid the tackler, recovered my balance from a healthy blow that didn't quite knock me off my feet, and looked down field to see the ball float into Calvin's arms on about their 30-yard line. Well ahead of his defender, he scampered over the goal line for a touchdown.

The crowd recovered from their shock and surprise and exploded into cheering. I saw my family screaming and my brother, Lynn, laughing for all he was worth, clapping his hands and throwing back his head in amazement. The Rosy Red Bomb had worked, and we all felt a resurgence of hope.

As we attempted the extra point, Max Jack was thrown for a loss, prompting an energetic round of heckling from the opposition who felt they'd pulled a fast one on us. We kicked off again and, as before, their offense marched barbarically play by play down the field. The rest of the game was a repeat of what had happened during the opening ten minutes. After they punished us with good-old American hard-hitting football, they'd find themselves within scoring distance and we somehow managed to get back the ball. We'd attempt a few various plays, but it was soon evident that such plays weren't gaining ground. Invariably, we'd return to the "Rosy Red Bomb." It became our standard formation. We even picked up short yardage by running variations of the same play. Defenders were positioning themselves so deep at times that our receivers were practically assured of a twenty- or thirty-yard completion by doubling back. It seemed to get better as the game progressed. Our running game also opened up.

During halftime, word got around the base about what was happening. By the time the game was over, quite a crowd of additional airmen, other family members, and students had gathered. Our linemen were developing confidence and played harder on defense as a result of our success on offense. We got plenty of practice and experience that day. Everyone discovered that skill and agility could match and beat size and strength. We also realized our team spirit and enthusiasm were important ingredients to success. Team confidence surged as each quarter came to an end.

As the clock ran out we were leading, 32 to 0. It had been a miracle! *Stars and Stripes* wouldn't have believed it. It was hard for *us* to believe it, but we'd won the game and felt thrilled with the victory. We'd realized our potential and developed creative moves and plays to defeat an intimidating opponent. We won!

From this experience, I learned that a well-prepared offense will always help defeat a superior opponent. Not only does this maxim apply to the challenges of our daily lives, it applies to the struggle to which many American have enlisted in the face of dominating and imposing political philosophies running rampant and unchecked in our schools, our media, our government, and sometimes inside the walls of our own homes.

This book will focus heavily on the principle of preparing an effective offense. As Coach Lewis taught us repeatedly,

"The best offense is always our best defense." In the current political climate it may feel like you are *always* playing defense. That's when it's time to throw a few "Rosy Red Bombs" and other power plays to regain momentum.

In my battle for the presidency of the United States, I expect opposition far more intimidating than the Army's football team of Orleans, France. No worries. In my playbook I have a few unexpected "Rosy Red Bombs" in store for my opponents. And I fully expect to use them.

BILL BRADLEY

That same year in England, we also had a great basketball team and nearly won the All-European Basketball Tournament. The other four seniors included Buff Blount, Calvin Bradley, Max Jack and Bob Toombs. We dominated every team, including the base team that had quite a few college players. In the spring, Brandon Toolin and I won fourth in our doubles at the All-European Tennis Championship.

During my CHS high school graduation ceremony, I was privileged to sit on stage right behind Bill Bradley, my basketball hero. By 1965, he'd been named as the NCAA Player of the Year and played with the American basketball team at the Tokyo Olympics. He turned down professional teams to attend Oxford University as a Rhodes Scholar. He delivered an inspiring speech about being all we can be. After graduation, Buff Blount and I drove him back to his apartment at Oxford. He invited us in and we talked for a while about basketball, education, patriotism and service. Great people inspire greatness in others.

Chapter 3

Roots of an American

A LEADER ON AND OFF THE FIELD

A public stand for principles and standards is vital for public servants prepared for confrontation, challenged popularity or retribution. The following event had been recorded in the journal of my dear friend, Kevin Rarick. His journal reads as follows:

"We all know how it is to be in High School and how many 'cliques' or select groups develop. We also know how it is to be on the outside looking in and wanting very much to be accepted. May I tell you of a High School experience dealing with that situation and how a person handled the situation that changed my life?

"I was a senior at Central High School in England and had just finished football practice. I felt very good about how I was doing and wanted very much to be accepted by the 'in group' (the best athletes). As things go, the locker room was steaming, sweaty bodies were everywhere, and the talk began to deteriorate into this conquest and that about women. I never got into those conversations, but would listen without comment.

"While I was dressing, the new guy in school from Blackfoot, Idaho (wherever that was) stood up and stunned the group by saying, 'You guys shouldn't talk about girls like that. They are special, and if you mess around you could get diseases that could affect you all your lives.' Such was the profound advice that an

American from Blackfoot, Idaho imparted to a group of youth in London, England. You could have heard a pin drop! Then they began to jeer and shrug off their embarrassment by making fun (of what I had to say?). The funny thing was the conversation changed and no more low talk took place."

A few moments after this, Kevin Rarick sat down beside me and said, "I always wanted to say that, but had never had the courage to do it."

ROTTERDAM, HOLLAND

That summer after my senior year I got a job with the Dutch division of Chicago Bridge & Iron in Rotterdam, Holland. After school was out, I caught the train to Dover and took the ferry to Calais, France. This was the first real experience I'd ever had living among people whose first language was not English. In fact, these "bull gangs" represented numerous nationalities and languages, including Dutch, German, Spanish, French, Portuguese, Italian, Arabic and nations of Africa. I worked on the construction of three oil tanks side by side for $1.25 per hour, plus a living allowance. When I started working, the first tank was under partial construction with the first ring on the base. The second tank only had the floor plates tack welded into place and the third tank had not yet begun. At the end of the summer, the first tank was almost completed, including the floating lid or roof.

We were called "bull gangs" after the heavy, long cone-shaped bull pin that held the huge metal plates in place while they were being welded. They also secured the scaffolding to the inside walls as the rings of metal were added on top of one another, forming the tank wall.

Laborers generally only spoke a few words of each other's languages. My job was to understand the Dutch foreman's instructions and then to make sure the workers knew what they needed to do for the day. This allowed the foreman to visit all three tanks and do a better job of supervision. Gradually, I learned the language of the bull gang and how to get the job done. It was dangerous work with long, hard days, but it was also very satisfying.

This experience reemphasized certain values that had sustained me all of my life—that all people, from all cultures, are basically the same. These men loved their families and wanted the best for them. Most were genuinely good people and wanted a fair shake from the world. They had their strengths and their weaknesses. They were like me, which was a refreshing confirmation for a boy from Idaho.

At the end of the summer, I returned to England and hitchhiked through central and southern England to see Stonehenge, Bath and other places I'd read about. I proceeded on through Liverpool to southern Ireland to kiss the Blarney Stone high in the castle wall outside of Cork. That night, I slept in the hayloft of a barn beside the Blarney Castle. When I woke up, the castle was floating above a cloud of fog and framed by the upper doors of the barn. It was magnificent, and I experienced a moment of awe and inspiration.

A few days later, I flew out of the Limerick Airport and arrived in New York City on August 26, 1966. During the flight, I pondered the many unique and life changing things I had experienced during my past year in Europe.

HOME TO THE UNITED STATES

As we circled to land, and again when I stepped off the airplane onto American soil, I was filled with patriotism and gratitude for this wonderful land and a euphoric sense of pride that I was blessed to be a part of it. I felt so humbled, so full of love, that I wanted to kneel and kiss the ground. The sight of the Statue of Liberty brought a surge of emotion into my heart.

It was Saturday afternoon and all the banks were closed. In those days there was no such thing as an ATM. All of my money was in English currency or English travelers checks. With only two American dimes in my pocket I decided there wasn't any reason to wait around in New York City. I could be half way to Idaho by the time the banks opened on Monday morning.

After buying two packages of chewing gum and getting a good, long drink of cold water from a drinking fountain, I walked out of the airport and began hitchhiking home. Traffic on that sunny afternoon was headed toward the airport exit, so I began walking in that direction. The first car I waved at picked me up. The driver was a young black man about my age. He was a recent Vietnam War veteran, recovering from a bullet wound in the chest. The bullet had penetrated the sternum and lodged next to his heart. He told me he was one of the lucky ones. Many others in his platoon didn't survive. It caused me to wonder if such drama lay ahead for me. I was of draft age and might be called up to go to Vietnam at any time.

My host driver was headed for Philadelphia, but didn't know the way. He'd apparently picked me up hoping I could help him with directions. Together we sighted the first New Jersey license plate and began following that car. We talked continually and thoroughly enjoyed our ride together. He had struggled with evil and death on a daily basis, but had occasionally witnessed goodness that made it all worthwhile. I admired him and even felt a little envious. He was a genuinely good person and had sincere faith in God.

Other people who gave me rides were very kind to me and shared their food, philosophy, and war stories going back to

Korea and World Wars I and II. I arrived home in Blackfoot four days to the hour after I left the airport.

Hitchhiking across the country was to be the first of many such trips across this country in years to come. At the time, I traveled on faith and the good will of others. From beginning to end, I was blessed with success. It was the 60s, and the majority of Americans had generous hearts. Fear of violence or mugging or serial killers never came to my mind. I never felt threatened or endangered, nor did the drivers show any evidence of being frightened of me.

After my return to Idaho, I enjoyed a happy, but short-lived, reunion with my family. Then I left home once more, this time to attend Brigham Young University in Provo, Utah for my first year of college.

My dream, of course, was to play college basketball. Despite my successes and some degree of talent on the football field, my firm conviction was that future success in sports would be on the basketball court. Since BYU had already handed out their basketball scholarships for that year, I was offered a football scholarship. I played second-string quarterback and could run and throw the ball well. Earlier, as a high school junior, I had been measured to throw a football 96 yards. Nevertheless, I still felt my future was in basketball. I agreed to play football at BYU with a promise from the coach that I could try out for the basketball team when the season began.

We had a successful football season. During the last two weeks, I was suiting up for both football and basketball practice. On the last day of football practice the head coach learned that I was practicing with the basketball team and put an end to this activity. He told the basketball coach in no uncertain terms that I was on a football scholarship and not to allow me back on the basketball floor. I felt very discouraged. Some might feel the potential of becoming a quarterback or defensive halfback for BYU should have been impossible to bypass, but I decided life had a different plan for me to follow, and I decided to find out what that plan was.

AN LDS CHURCH MISSION

There were three options facing me at this turning point. I was 1-A in the draft for Vietnam, and the war was escalating. There were several levels of the draft, and 1-A was at the top of the list, with all names potentially being called up at any time. I had no qualms about serving my country if my number came up. Another option was to transfer to another college where I could play basketball. The third option was to serve a mission for The Church of Jesus Christ of Latter-day Saints. In those days there were quotas for a certain number of young men who could serve missions. The quota for my congregation in Blackfoot was already filled. Later, I was told someone in Salt Lake City decided not to go. Miraculously, I was privileged to receive a mission call to serve in the New England States Mission.

I entered the Missionary Training Center in Salt Lake City, Utah, where I memorized the six missionary lessons used at that time to teach the Gospel to others. With my training complete, I traveled with Elder Stewart Crane to Boston. The assistants to the mission president picked us up after dark, took us to the mission home for a bowl of soup, and let us sleep. Early the next morning, after breakfast, we were whisked to the bus station to journey to our assigned proselyting areas. Elder Crane went his way south and I went north. My first area was in Plattsburg, upstate New York.

The New England Mission in 1968 included the states of Massachusetts, Rhode Island, Vermont, New Hampshire and

Maine. It also included the Canadian maritime provinces of New Brunswick, Nova Scotia, Prince Edward's Island and Newfoundland. Greenland was also included, but there were no missionaries assigned there. The four missionaries serving in Newfoundland were transferred only in the spring and fall.

(Today, with the growth of the LDS Church, these areas have been divided into many missions, each with an average of 200 to 250 missionaries, all serving on a volunteer basis and financed by funds they have saved since they were young children or by help from their families or home congregations, etc. Young men are eligible to serve for two years and young women for eighteen months. The young men serve when they are 18 years old and young women at age 19. There are also thousands of older missionaries; many of them married couples who serve in a wide range of capacities. Most people, when they think of LDS missionaries, imagine young, clean-cut men riding bicycles or knocking on doors. They may serve in poverty or disaster stricken parts of the world, helping communities rebuild and providing refugees with the necessities of life. Some serve missions updating computer records or helping individuals overcome addictions. These critical functions and duties apply to *all* LDS missionaries—to build, to uplift, to motivate and to inspire people to seek a better life.)

During the two years I served a mission, I experienced much rejection and ridicule for my beliefs, but no physical harm. I learned to plan, pray, work hard, teach, listen, and communicate. I learned about faith, courage, dedication, perseverance, and to follow the example of Jesus Christ regardless of what others do. I experienced miracles. I learned how to help others make and keep commitments. These years were an invaluable training ground for the rest of my life. I served under the tutelage of two great men who were my mission presidents, men who I esteem as two of the greatest leaders in my church. Their examples and influence continues to inspire me today. I learned how to better communicate, not judge others and to treat people fairly. I learned how I would serve my future family. It was the foundation for success I would later achieve in multiple areas of my life.

While so many others of my generation followed different paths, I spent these preparatory years sincerely serving others the best way I knew how. What I learned was eloquently stated by my father in several letters he wrote to me during that period. Sometimes it's when we are caught up in soul-stretching service that we learn our most valuable lessons.

On June 8, 1968 my father wrote, "Time is tremendously vital; in fact time is part of eternity; and eternity is now . . . Phooey to procrastination."

It was my privilege to meet many marvelous people while living and serving in Maine, Massachusetts, New Hampshire and Vermont. During the first week of July, 1968, we visited Maria Von Trapp at the Von Trapp Family Lodge in Stowe, Vermont. It was an honor to meet the woman who'd inspired the movie, *The Sound of Music*. As previously stated, this movie and music had inspired me and cultivated deep feelings of patriotism. Meeting her and discussing her feelings of good and bad, right and wrong, and sheer determination gave me more determination to climb my highest mountains. I'm still inspired each time I hear the words to the famous song *Climb Every Mountain* by Richard Rogers:

> *Climb every mountain, search high and low,*
> *Follow every byway, every path you know.*
> *Climb every mountain, ford every stream,*
> *Follow every rainbow, 'Till you find your dream.*

A dream that will need all the love you can give,
Every day of your life for as long as you live.

On December 28, 1968, my father wrote in a letter to me: "Control temper. No quarreling. These days we have too many men of science and too few men of God. Earthly existence is a test. Spiritually, our true aim is consciousness of victory over self and communion with the infinite."

Most people with a few decades of experience under their belt readily recognize the value that sacrifice and service can have in shaping someone's destiny and helping them focus on what's most important. Such experience can be gained in the military, the Red Cross, or any other organization whose objective is to make the world better or safer. Service to others changes the human soul and molds our eternal potential.

At any moment during my two years as a missionary I might have been called up to active duty and been sent to Vietnam. If drafted, I would have served and done my best. Service has been the guiding principle of my life, and will continue to be as President of the United States.

Near the end of my mission my father wrote me a letter of profound impact. Of course virtually all parents love their children. Often they have a difficult time expressing it, but when they do, it can cause a fountain of confidence to well up inside that makes us believe we are capable of anything; that no challenge is too great for us to overcome. These thoughts inflamed my heart and still burn there now. Here is part of that letter:

March 4, 1969:

"As I survey your near twenty-one years of progress, training and services, I'm convinced that whatever I may have done well you can do better and are capable of doing so much better. My life will

look rather elementary by comparison. This is as it should be in practically every area of activity. Society is now in high gear and whereas I traveled a few miles, met few people, and accomplished little, you shall travel far, meet multitudes and accomplish unlimited good. Leadership everywhere reflects tremendous opportunities, training, and possibilities and I think your potential is high. Positions, wealth or fame means little but true leadership in church, state, or vocation involves recognition of responsibilities, rendering of helpful service, and in earning an honest living. Work is still a good word. A challenge for you to live up to your potential may not be the most tactful or diplomatic way to conclude my letter . . . but my prayers are that you will do just that. I'm proud to claim you as a son."

The pride my father expressed in me, his son, is exceeded only by the love I still feel for this intelligent, but humble, hard-working man of God—my father.

Chapter 4

Crossroads

BASKETBALL AND COLLEGE

One of the last people I had the opportunity to teach on my mission was a hockey player from Boston College. After a missionary discussion in Cambridge, we drove him home in the mission president's car. I asked him about BC's basketball team and he added that Bob Cousey was their head coach. It was getting dark, just then we turned off Commonwealth Avenue through the front gate. I was amazed at how beautiful the campus was. It reminded me of the beautiful buildings of Oxford and Cambridge universities in England where I lived a few years before. St. Mary's Hall on the left inspired me and the Bapts Library on the right had beautiful stained windows and looked like a large cathedral. At that moment, I decided that I would someday return and attend Boston College.

After my church mission I felt as if I could do anything I set my mind to. I was about to go home, my whole life ahead of me, a hundred dreams buzzing in my head, and I had a strong feeling that I had a great destiny to fulfill. The question was, which destiny was I going to pursue?

God has always placed people in my path for a purpose. The week before I left my mission in Boston to return to Idaho, I played basketball with some Harvard MBA students, including Nolan D. Archibald, who'd been a great player himself. During a rest, he asked me if I'd ever considered playing college ball. I answered that it had been my dream since I was old enough to dribble. He personally interceded and spoke to the right people. Before the day was over I was offered a scholarship to play basketball at Dixie Junior College in southern Utah. Days later, I was on a plane to the town of St. George.

By the time I arrived in St. George, the school semester had already begun and basketball season was getting underway. For the next six months my entire life was devoted to studies, practice, and games. This schedule took up virtually every moment of my time. Sundays were truly a welcome day of rest. Even though it was the most difficult regimen I'd experienced, I progressed more and got higher grades than at any other time. Mine was one of the forty-three names to appear on Dixie College's High Honor Role with a 3.75 or better while carrying 15 credit hours or more. This would have been a difficult achievement even if I hadn't spent so much time on the basketball court.

I started the season very much out of shape. I fouled a lot because I was trying too hard. My first aggressive encounter was with Doug Bailey from Delta, Utah. Afterwards, Doug and I became close friends and remain so to this day. The Dixie basketball team had a good season. This year proved to be the beginning of an outstanding winning tradition that led Dixie to several national championships and tournament trophies in a number of sports.

Even so, at the end of the year, I felt impelled to transfer to Boston College in Chestnut Hill, Massachusetts, a Catholic school that had a very challenging academic program. They also, of great appeal to me, had a basketball team on which I hoped to play.

My father's advice had always had a big influence on me. I explained to my parents my ambitions and plans for how I intended to pay tuition at Boston College with a possible walk-on scholarship. I showed my father my budget and asked if he'd be there to help me out financially if I needed it. In his thoughtful, but steady voice, he said to me, "Well, Dale, I'll tell you like I told your older brother, Lynn, when he asked the same question. 'If you want to go to school badly enough, I'm sure you'll find a way.'" It was indeed a sobering statement. As I've thought back over the years, it was the best thing my father could have done. Soon, I was off to Boston with very little to sustain me besides extraordinary faith and confidence that all would work out.

Boston College had not had transfer students except for their Jesuit priests, who sometimes transferred from one Jesuit school to another. However, they agreed to consider my application. I filled out all the necessary paperwork and began the long process of waiting. I had a series of interviews with Father Walsh, the Head of Admissions, and several others. He invited me to sit in a nearby waiting room while he and the admissions board went into another room to discuss my case and make their final decision.

During that intense, hour-long wait, a priest happened to enter the waiting room. I stood up to introduce myself and firmly shook his hand. He introduced himself as Reverend Sidney MacNeil of the Society of Jesus. He was, unbeknownst to me, an Admissions Officer whose usual responsibility was to interview prospective students for their freshman year. Because I was a transfer student, I wasn't expected to interview with him. Nevertheless, we sat together for a time and had an enjoyable chat. In response to his many questions, I told him about my family, my Mormon religious background, and about my interest in school.

At the end of our "interview" he took me into his office and gave me a book and some other literature about Boston College. I thanked him and told him that I would keep it and read it. He looked up at me and said, "You know, I think I like you." I responded, "You know, I think I like you, too." That was the beginning of a long and very dear friendship. He invited me to go back to the waiting room while he spoke to the other administrators. Father Walsh soon emerged and announced that I would be accepted to BC, but there would have to be some additional paperwork. Not being used to having transfer students, they weren't quite sure what to do with me. To his credit, Father Walsh felt it was time their entry policies were adjusted, and he promised that I would be allowed to enroll for the fall semester. The school did not, however, offer me a scholarship. I would have to pay tuition. I would also have to find a place to live and find a way to pay for it.

The following year, on April 13, 1971, Father MacNeil wrote: "From the first time I met you, I was immensely impressed by your utter goodness." As a tribute to him, I want to mention that he was from Southborough, Massachusetts, and had earned his bachelor's and master's degrees from Boston College before entering the Society of Jesus. He had been assigned to the Jesuit Mission in Baghdad, Iraq, where he befriended many students and helped them receive scholarships and grants to study in the U.S. He later served as Assistant Director of Admissions at BC and chaplain at the Veterans' Administration Medical Center in West Roxbury until he retired. He died in 1987 while I was living out of the country.

BOSTON "MARATHON"

This marathon refers not to the runner's race, but to the financial trials that I endured and overcame as I sought higher education at Boston College. You see, I had it all worked out. I'd started a business venture with some buddies while I was at Dixie College in Utah and was just *certain* that its success would cover any and all tuition needs in Boston. The business agreement with my partners had been established on a handshake. I knew nothing about contracts or finances or accounting. We all relied on a great deal of trust. To make a long story short, things did not turn out as expected, and I found myself with no scholarship, no extra funding, and no prospects for financing my tuition beyond the first semester.

My parents were naturally concerned about my ability to work, study, and also play basketball without a scholarship. On September 11, 1970, my father wrote: "Personally I think a financially forced drop-out at the end of one semester would be more disappointing than you realize. If my judgment and prayers mean anything, you better weigh things pretty carefully for a long range plan before you put any money on the line."

It was purely an act of faith that I pursued my ambitions unabated. I found housing and entered classes the following week. I had several housemates, including Neizki Keflu (Niki) from Ethiopia and Cheng Chen Lin (he had chosen Mike for his English name) from Taiwan. Niki was a son of an Ethiopian nobleman and had spent four years studying political economics in Russia. Mike was studying for a master's degree in chemistry. His father owned a chemical and plastics factory in Taiwan.

I must say that one of the main reasons I went to Boston College was to play basketball for my idol, Bob Cousey. He was the greatest basketball player of his day and was coaching at Boston College the year before. After I enrolled in school, I went to the gym to introduce myself as a walk-on player. To my disappointment, I learned that Cousey had left for Cincinnati to coach a professional basketball team.

Chuck Dailey was the new coach. Coach Daily gave me a chance and offered to let me try out for the team. I did get on the team, although I didn't play much. After a Christmas holiday tournament, I broke my nose in practice.

To pay for my expenses, I worked in the cafeteria and at the Meyer's Parking Lot downtown. Sometimes I'd come home cold, wet, and exhausted to the bone. There just wasn't enough time to study and also get the rest I needed to play basketball at the level required. During this time I caught the flu and became very ill and weak. This was also the time that some of the bills came due for the failed business venture in Utah. It was evident that I had seen as much of Boston College as I would that year. I returned home to earn money for the next fall semester.

A NEW HOME

The time finally came for me to go back to Boston College. I was determined that this was my time to prove myself. I would be signing up for some of the hardest classes in the pre-med program. These classes included physics, calculus, trigonometry, biology, and organic chemistry.

My landlady had rented out my old room for double what I'd paid the year before. However, we agreed to $45 per month for an attic room full of junk if I raked leaves, shoveled snow, and cleaned out and fixed up the room. I promptly repaired and painted the attic. I got the furniture from the basement and painted it also. My attic bedroom became the nicest room in the house.

The day classes started, my landlady told me she now required $90 a month for my room. I was heartsick and pleaded for her to keep to our bargain. We both knew that all the rooms were rented and there wouldn't be any more available. She held firm as I left for class. On the way I passed a beautiful Tudor home. After class I felt inspired to knock on the door to see if they would consider renting a room. Mrs. Judy Cutter answered and miraculously showed a willingness to hear my story. The inside of the Cutter's home was elegant. She invited me to return later that evening to discuss my situation with her husband Harold. I went home excited and felt I had been inspired to approach them. Just as I returned to my attic room and lay down on my bed, the landlady's son knocked on the door and came in. He insisted that I pay $90 and reminded me that I would never find another place to live at this late date.

I returned to the Cutter's home with feelings of desperation. Mrs. Cutter explained that they only had one maid's room available. She and her husband asked if I would be willing to stay around the house on weekends if they were gone. I told her I would be happy to do so and that I'd also do yard work, rake leaves, shovel snow, and whatever else was needed as I was in an urgent position. They politely listened to me. I explained a few times that I could only pay $45 per month.

Mr. Harold Cutter finally said they felt comfortable with me moving in, but he didn't want my money. He said it would be a mutually beneficial arrangement. They invited me to come back the next day so they could have the room ready for me. I went home, slept soundly, and the next morning moved my things over to their house. When I went back to pay my landlady for the rent I owed her, she was very angry that I'd moved away. I apologized and reminded her that she had left me no alternative. It was her decision to raise my rent that had brought about the change. She was mad and told me that I should be ashamed of myself to leave her without a renter. I had not thought of it before, but while there were no rooms for me in town, neither were there any renters for her because all the students were settled in. I apologized, and that was the last time I saw her.

My new home was a testimony to me that God had answered my prayers and had provided for my needs. The Cutters blessed me throughout my stay at their home. Not only did they refuse any rent, they paid me for things for which I hadn't asked payment. Mr. Cutter would often give me $20 or $50 dollars. When I said, "No, I can't take this," he would force it into my hand or my pocket, saying, "Please don't embarrass me."

I love the whole Cutter family, especially their oldest son, Steve. He was such a mature young man. They made me part of their family. They included me in many of their family activities. We had pillow fights, and they often invited me to special events. I was able to help them host their guests at a Bar Mitzvah, Passover meals, and special dinner parties. All of these were very elegant affairs.

Some of my most carefree and exciting ocean experiences were enjoyed while visiting the Cutters in their home in West Yarmouth on Cape Cod. At Christmas time they got a tree for me so I could celebrate Christmas and wouldn't be homesick. Mrs. Cutter's mother was a bit upset, but Judy told her mother it was a Hanukkah bush.

My mother wrote to me on October 5, 1971: "I do hope you will be happy where you live now and that you can make yourself useful and helpful sufficiently to abundantly earn the love and appreciation from those folks and I'm sure our Heavenly Father will continue to bless you if you continue to be a good boy."

During that year, I was determined to prove something to myself. I applied for some of the hardest classes in the pre-med program. I'd have to study very hard. Receiving a "C" in any of those classes would end any possibility of acceptance into medical school. In particular, a "C" in organic chemistry was known as the "kiss of death."

I studied faithfully and did reasonably well in all of my classes. Honestly, I had little time for anything *but* studying and working to support myself. Most of my evenings and all day Saturdays, I worked as a supervisor in the cafeteria, overseeing twenty or thirty other students.

In my first semester, I got a "B-" in organic chemistry. Approximately 60 out of 120 students received "C's," and a great number received "D's." The remainder simply flunked out. The second semester was even *more* competitive because there were fewer students. My grade dropped from a B- to a C+, even though I felt like I'd understood the material, had studied very hard, and tested better than during the first semester. I felt sure that I deserved a better grade. Looking back, it was an invaluable learning experience and helped me develop a sense of mental discipline and study habits that I never forgot. I don't regret the experience, but I have to admit that it was a very busy and difficult year.

On February 3, 1972, Father McNeil wrote the following letter of recommendation to Mr. John Walsh of the Boston College Housing Office. I believe this letter tipped the scales and got me the job.

"Pursuant to my oral recommendation, I wish to offer a written testimonial in favor of Mr. Dale H Christensen, who is applying to be a Resident Assistant. For the past two years I have been Dale's counselor. In all my 33 years of dealing with students I have not met a student with better character. He combines high moral probity with great sympathy for anyone who has problems and difficulties. A strong talent for leadership is mellowed by an understanding flexibility. I cannot even imagine a person who would give better quiet edification to students than Dale. Due to his missionary experience (required by the Mormon religion), he is two years older than the average age in his class, and six years

older than freshmen. Dale, as you know, has a commanding but gentle appearance. He is six feet three inches tall and weighs about 190 pounds. Dale's resume is indeed interesting. He is mature far beyond his years."

DISCERNING TRUTH FROM ERROR

In my history class, we were aggressively taught that Social Darwinism and Marxist Socialism evolved from revolution and the struggle of the exploited masses taking power from the rich minority. I believed that America provided all its citizens with the opportunity for not only religious freedom, but the opportunity to acquire wealth and power by realizing the "American Dream."

Most students in my class believed that this was no longer possible. They believed the "Establishment" had gobbled up all wealth and power for themselves. It might seem hypocritical, since most of the young men and women came from very wealthy families. It seemed some of my fellow students sincerely despised their "capitalistic" parents. Ironically, after graduation, most of these same individuals shaved their beards and long hair and replaced them with a tie and business attire. They followed their parents and quickly became the "Capitalist Pigs" they'd previously despised.

During one study session of this class, I boldly declared, "My father was a farmer and a teacher. I come from a poor, hardworking family, but I believe that if I study and work hard I can be as rich, famous, and powerful as anyone else." When they told me I was dreaming, I stated that, "Some of them might appreciate their education a lot more if they had to pay for it and not had it handed to them on a silver platter."

That evoked some sharp critical reactions. Our assistant professor suggested that I represent the Adam Smith point of view for the following day's discussion. At the time, I didn't really understand much about Adam Smith, but I did have strong feelings about the American Dream.

Someone quoted from our text material where it described the rise of the proletariat to the position of the position of the ruling class and political supremacy. This was to be accomplished by following the steps outlined in Karl Marx's *Communist Manifesto*, taking capital from the bourgeoisie and centralizing all instruments of production in the hands of the state. The blueprint was as follows:

1. Abolition of private property.
2. A heavy progressive or graduated income tax.
3. Abolition of all rights of inheritance.
4. Confiscation of the property of all emigrants and rebels.
5. Centralization of credit in the hands of the State, by means of a national bank.
6. Centralization of the means of communication and transport in the hands of the State.
7. Establishment of industrial armies, etc.

They used this to justify the social revolution that had occurred in Russia. My response was, "This is a description of what's happening in our own country today. Whether or not it is good for the individual or the nation is another question." The bell rang and the class was over. I was troubled by the discussion, but couldn't put my finger on what had bothered me most.

The next day, as we gathered in the large amphitheater in McEwen Hall, our professor stood at the front of class, ready to deliver his lecture. He was a dapper-looking gentleman with a sharp goatee, much like the Soviet socialist leader

Vladimir Lenin. He launched into a subtle attack on America's imperialistic aggressions, referring to the situation at the end of the Spanish-American War in 1898, when the Philippines were taken from Spanish rule and awarded to the United States. In an interview, U.S. President William McKinley stated:

> *"I have been criticized a good deal about the Philippines, but I don't deserve it. The truth is, I didn't want the Philippines, and when they came to us, as a gift from the gods, I did not know what to do with them. When the Spanish war broke out, Dewey was at Hong Kong, and I ordered him to go to Manila, and he had to; because, if defeated, he had no place to refit on that side of the globe, and if the Dons were victorious they would likely cross the Pacific and ravage our Oregon and California coasts. And so he had to destroy the Spanish fleet, and did it. But that was as far as I thought then.*
>
> *"When next I realized that the Philippines had dropped into our lap, I confess that I did not know what to do with them. I sought counsel from all sides —Democrats as well as Republicans—but got little help. I thought first we would take only Manila; then Luzon; then other islands, perhaps all. I walked the floor of the White House night after night until midnight; and I am not ashamed to tell you, gentlemen, that I went down on my knees and prayed to Almighty God for light and guidance more than one night. And one night late it came to me this way. I don't know how it was, but it came: (1) That we could not give them back to Spain—that would be cowardly and dishonorable; (2) that we could not turn them over to France or Germany—that would be bad business and discreditable; (3) that we could not leave them to themselves—they were unfit for self-government and would soon have anarchy and misrule over there worse than Spain's was; and (4) that there was nothing left for us to do but to take them all, and to educate the Filipinos, and uplift and civilize and Christianize them, and, by*

God's grace, do the very best we could by them, as our fellowmen for whom Christ died.

"And then I went to bed, and went to sleep, and slept soundly, and next morning I sent for the chief engineer of the War Department (our map-maker) and told him to put the Philippines on the map of the United States (pointing to a large map on the wall of his office); and there they are, and there they will stay while I am President!"

Our professor boldly called President McKinley a liar for saying that God had inspired him. At that moment I knew that something was terribly amiss in our class. I raised my hand and was called on to comment. I asked the professor why he thought President McKinley was a liar.

He said, "Because there is no God, and he just used that as an excuse to justify to the American people and the world's obvious imperialistic aggression."

I responded. "But he may have sincerely believed that he had been inspired." At least that was how the account had struck me. "We can't judge him as an intentional liar. Maybe *he* believed in God even if *you* don't."

"Yes." was his response, "Almost all bourgeoisies sincerely believe in God. This is the very evil that is the cause of today's capitalistic imperialism and aggression on the weaker peoples of the world."

I countered, "It sounds to me like you're advocating socialism instead of just teaching us about it."

He responded without reservation. "Yes, I am a socialist and advocate it as the ultimate solution."

As he spoke those words, I felt the cold reality of what he was doing. During the moments he spoke and those following while he waited for my rebuttal, I felt well up inside me a solid understanding and distinction between the truth and error of what was being taught. This inspiration warned me to carefully sift out that which was not correct. So many things came into blazing focus.

My next statement was to the point. "Now, I see things much more clearly," I began. "I hope the rest of these students can see what you are trying to do. It's one thing to learn about communism, but it's quite another thing to be taught and convinced that it is a better system than democracy as our forefathers envisioned it under this republic."

The 125 other students in the amphitheater stared at me wide-eyed and listened without interruption during our brief debate. After a long silence, the professor asked if he could continue with the other topics of the lecture, which he did.

When class was over, I went down to the podium and told him I didn't want to be offensive, and I certainly didn't want him to lower my grade because of my impassioned statements. I told him that I enjoyed his class, which was true. Some of the best classes I've ever had in life were those that forced me to rethink my convictions and boil down those principles that I really believed were true. I told the professor that I had felt compelled to express my opinions that day. He smiled politely and agreed that it was important that we recognize one another's differences.

Since then, I have felt that inner voice—call it the Holy Spirit, call it intuition, call it whatever you want—but I've relied upon it countless times to confirm truths in many areas of study and observation.

It's my firm belief that anyone can hear the same voice or rely upon the same inspiration. We are all promised: "Ask, and it shall be given you; seek, and ye shall find; knock, and it shall be opened unto you" (Mathew 7:7). So the key is, when in doubt, focus upon a Higher Source for intelligence and direction. In today's secular world, this principle—the same principle expressed by President McKinley—has often been ignored or even frowned upon. My own formula is the same one used by President Abraham Lincoln: "Pray as if all depended upon God, then act as if all depended upon me." This formula for life has never yet failed me.

Grandfather
Christian H. Christensen

Grandmother
Bena Marie Frogner

Grandfather
William Thorton

Grandmother
Esther Swift

Father
Irven Christensen

Mother
Esther Thornton

Irven & Esther
Wedding Day

Irven & Ester
50th Wedding Anniversary

Dale (1 yr) with Sister Dian and Brother Art   2 Years Old

Father and Son   Our Growing Family

Dale - 4 Years Old   High School Graduation

1951   1964

Dale Christensen

Irven Christensen Family - Reunion 1973

CHS Footbal

Tennis Doubles

CHS Basketball Team

CHS Basketball

CHS Basketball

Mission Maine
Capital Building

Maria Von Trapp
in Vermont

Boston College

Riding Maureen at the Kelly Black Angus Ranch

Chapter 5

Shaping My Destiny

HITCH-HIKING

Over the next five years, while going to college in the East, I hitched-hiked back and forth across the United States many times. There were always wonderful people who helped me as far as they could, frequently offering me something to eat and telling me the stories of their lives. I loved it, as I didn't have the money to travel any other way to get to school or return home for holidays or summer vacations. Whenever I wasn't in a car or truck, I was walking. I've done it enough times to be able to say that I've walked across the United States at least once.

LOVE OF MY LIFE

Thus far at college, I'd attempted to win the hearts of several young women, but with little or no success. With one, I felt quite miserable. Again, my father was often the most dependable source of insight on this matter. In January of 1971 he wrote to me the following:

> *"Very seriously, Dale, if on a dating basis a gal can and would deliberately or unwittingly upset a fellow to the point where he can't study, then he better seriously consider how he's going to handle a like situation after marriage when, as a doctor or businessman, he is away so much and everything seems to contribute to a problem.*

A wife must help, support and encourage. As Paul said, 'Be not unequally yoked.' All these thoughts have nothing to do with any particular gal, but I'm wondering if you need to survey your own needs, feelings and desires and see if you can find someone who complements your personality and fits the wife's responsibilities that you feel you need—and remember 'What care I how fair she be if she think not well of me.' That, of course works, both ways."

What profound advice! As I consider the relationships I had with my parents, I'm all the more moved and humbled to think that they expended such extraordinary energy helping me become the man I am today.

The following autumn I attended an LDS church meeting called Stake Conference. Our stake president, L. Tom Perry, outlined a plan for the members of local congregations to choose various areas of their lives wherein they would be absolutely perfect for thirty days (i.e., paying 10 percent tithing, personal prayer, reading scriptures, etc.). President Perry promised great blessings by following this plan. When a leader like a stake president makes a promise of this magnitude, the congregation takes it very seriously.

I was a stake missionary, having little success in my assignment. I carefully selected the areas where I wanted to improve and made a personal commitment to be perfect in these things. During that month my efforts produced much fruit, but none compared to the blessing of meeting a certain young lady while visiting a friend in her Boston College dormitory room. As we spoke, in walked another beautiful co-ed. Her name was Mary-Jo Nanna. She needed help on a chemistry problem. Chemistry indeed! Though I didn't know it at the time, a chemical reaction was set off that night that would eventually lead to the most wonderful blessings of my life.

Mary-Jo was born in Mt. Vernon, New York, on May 14, 1953. She had dark hair and 100 percent Italian ancestry. When I met her she was not a member of the LDS faith, and she had many questions about religion and was searching for answers. I helped her with chemistry and then told her I was holding a tutoring session in a few days for a number of other students prior to an important exam. She came to the session held in my dorm room at Fitzpatrick Hall. As a resident assistant, I had a living room where students could meet.

Mary-Jo recalls that I was one of the few people on campus with short hair. She thought I was friendly and was the first person she'd ever met wearing cowboy boots. She asked if she could continue to study after everyone else had gone. However, I had a prior commitment to take the Cutter children out for pizza. As I was leaving, I asked if she would like to come along with us, but she wanted to stay and study.

While I was gone, she took a break from her work and looked over some of the religious books on the shelf above my desk. Later, I walked her back to her dormitory. She said, "By the books I saw above your desk, you must have religious feelings." I affirmed that I did, and she asked if she could come by sometime to discuss them because she had many questions. I told her she was welcome to come by anytime.

Days later we found ourselves having the first of many religious discussions. On that initial occasion we spoke for almost four hours. The most important message I had to present was my conviction that there was indeed a Savior of the world and that an acceptance of his Atonement was the most fundamental and important principal of God's plan for his children. I expressed my view that Christ had restored his church through living prophets. She was deeply impressed and soon expressed a sincere interest in learning more.

Mary-Jo explained that she'd felt a spiritual emptiness and a great longing for religious conviction. She explained that something was missing with her studies at Boston College. I asked her what it was that she wanted most in life. She gave what in those days—and perhaps more so today—was a surprising answer. She said that her greatest ambition was to be a wife and mother. Mary-Jo was the first girl I'd met since attending Boston College who admitted to such desires and feelings. All the other girls I'd met at BC seemed intent on becoming lawyers, doctors, business women, and professionals in one field or another.

I told her about my sister, who had graduated from Brigham Young University with the same lifetime goal. Dian had studied child development and family relations and received a Bachelor's Degree of Arts. Mary-Jo was so excited when she learned this that she went directly home that night and wrote a letter to BYU. She told them that she knew Dale Christensen (as if that would have a powerful impact on the admissions office). In short, she wanted to attend. She thought it was a small school, but soon learned that it had over 20,000 students. Shortly thereafter, and with only that letter of request and a scholarly GPA, she received a letter of acceptance.

When Mary-Jo went home for Thanksgiving she'd already expressed a desire to join the LDS faith. While she was home for the holiday weekend, she enthusiastically told her next door neighbor about the church she'd found. To her surprise, this neighbor informed her that she was already LDS and had been baptized seven years earlier. Despite this, to Mary-Jo's knowledge, neither the missionaries nor her neighbor had ever knocked on the Nanna family's front door to share the good news.

Mary-Jo's parents had strong Catholic roots, yet they never had any objection to their daughter's excitement about joining

The Church of Jesus Christ of Latter-day Saints. Her parents, along with her neighbor, even attended a special Thanksgiving program in the local Scarsdale New York LDS meetinghouse. Mary-Jo's mom had visited the New York World's Fair in the '60's and was very impressed with it and the Mormon Tabernacle Choir. Back at Boston College, while studying and having the missionary discussions, Mary-Jo invited the missionaries to teach some of her friends, who were also later baptized into the LDS Church.

In a letter home earlier that fall, after meeting Mary-Jo, I wrote to my parents that the missionary work at Boston College was picking up: "Guess what happened this week? A girl knocked on my door and asked to know more about my religion. She has now had two discussions and will be having more. She is really a special person and prepared to hear the Gospel. Her name is Mary-Jo Nanna. She may be the first person at BC to be baptized."

Even at that time I was unaware of the long-term nature of the relationship I was developing. I was trying to have faith and act according to my conscience.

Over the Christmas holidays Mary-Jo read the *Book of Mormon* and many related books. When she came back to school for finals, she accepted the invitation to be baptized and asked me to perform the baptism. I never dated any girls learning about my church. It's important to be careful when someone joins our faith that they are joining for the right reasons. Joining for any reason beyond personal conviction could lead to discouragement or backsliding. At this time, I didn't have romantic interest in Mary-Jo. We were dear friends, and I felt from the strength of her testimony that I was merely an instrument in the Lord's hands for bringing her to a state of religious conviction. This was confirmed when shortly after her baptism she moved more than 2000 miles away to attend Brigham Young University.

GOING TO POT

I had a difficult final semester at Boston College. Surprisingly, this had little to do with academics or my studies. In one of our last resident assistant meetings with the Housing Department, the administrators thought we should all know more about the harmful effects of drugs, etc. Alcoholism was discussed, and there was literature passed out on hard drugs such as heroin and cocaine. These were the days of "hippies" with an attitude that everything goes. More and more people were experimenting with drugs.

When the group brought up marijuana, one of the freer-spirited administrators thought we should know more about what we were discussing. He passed around a few joints for everyone in the room to sample. The conversation strangely transformed into something that resembled an invitation rather than a warning. Even though smoking and drinking were allowed on campus, I couldn't believe what I was witnessing. This was supposed to deter students from becoming involved in drugs? I was very disappointed, so I got up and left.

All that year I had forbidden pot parties to be held in the dorm. Now, with this latest example from the RAs, this rule was going to be all the more difficult to enforce. By the time I arrived home to my dorm, where I served as resident assistant, word had already spread across campus about what had occurred. The guys on my floor asked me what I was going to do, obviously wondering if my strict enforcement of the rules was going to continue.

I remained committed in my decision to steer clear of such substances and encourage others to do the same. Using addictive substances threaten our freedom of choice and sound judgment.

Then, as now, some people twisted the meaning of freedom to mean to be free to act irresponsibly or without regard for others. People were crying out for freedom to choose and freedom from bondage. The freedom they really wanted was the freedom to pursue a course of self-destruction. The whole premise of America is the idea of freedom, but many people today distort the meaning of freedom. I find it sad to watch people exercising their precious freedom to partake of substances inherently dangerous that will inhibit their free will and ability to choose. Such freedom cannot possibly be compared with the freedoms our forefathers fought so valiantly to provide and preserve. The whole concept seemed to me to be an oxymoron.

VISIONS, DECISIONS, AND MATRIMONY

Spring of my senior year left me having to make some monumental decisions. It was a difficult personal time. I'd gone to Boston with the long-term plan to go into the medical profession. I'd begun my studies with a strong desire to serve and heal people. Now I was beginning to have questions and new ideas about how I could best do that.

A trip home that spring with my friend, Dave Freitag, proved to be a life-changing experience. We drove Dave's convertible to visit our families in Utah, Idaho, and Maryland before heading back to Boston. As we traveled on Route I-70 through the breathtaking vistas of the Rocky Mountains of Colorado, we had the convertible top down and wrapped ourselves in blankets, with the heat turned up on high. We sang as loud as we could, over and over, John Denver's song "Rocky Mountain High."

I took my turn to drive so Dave could catch a glimpse of Pike's Peak, but the summit was covered in clouds. We continued eastward with the setting sun at our backs. Dave fell asleep and I drove most of the night across the rest of Colorado and most of Kansas. My mind was racing with thoughts. It was an illuminating night, indeed.

I don't recall much of the driving except stopping for gas, but I clearly remember my thoughts, impressions, and feelings. It was almost like a panoramic vision unfolding before me outlining the purpose of my life. When Dave woke up he began to talk about his own feelings of either medicine or dentistry. He'd studied business during his undergraduate years. Ironically, I'd devoted studies to the sciences, but I now had a great desire to study business and politics. The adrenalin was surging strongly in my veins. I boldly announced to Dave that someday I might even become a candidate for President of the United States.

That summer, my feelings for Mary-Jo evolved into something deeper than friendship. In late August, before I returned to Boston, I went to visit her at BYU. This time I'd be returning to Boston College to begin my MBA classes in the Carroll School of Management and then later study political science. Mary-Jo and I laughed heartily as I regaled her with my latest jokes and funny stories. By accident she said, "Oh, I just love you!" Surprised, I asked her to repeat what she had said. Embarrassed, she shyly and quietly said, "I love you."

Hours later I had the courage to make the same announcement to her. From that moment on I knew she was the girl I wanted to marry. The next day, I began my journey back east. I was half way across Nebraska when I realized I was going the wrong way. I was headed to Boston and Mary-Jo was in Utah.

One of my first stops in the East was to visit her family's summer lake house, Candlewood Lake Shores, in Brookfield, Connecticut. Her father was barbecuing chicken outside on the patio when I told him that I would like to make my friendship with Mary-Jo permanent. Dr. Nanna turned to me with a very pleasing smile and said, "Mother and I knew that the night we met you." He told me that during the meeting, he had leaned over to his wife and with tears in his eyes, pointed to me and said, "That's going to be our future son-in-law." Mrs. Nanna was excited for us and expressed her love and support.

Not everyone was excited by my plans to start a family. Later, I told Mrs. Cutter of my interest in Mary-Jo and a possible wedding. She exclaimed, "Dale, you're only a baby! Wait until you're finished with school and have your own business and home. Wait until you're at least thirty-one years old."

Mrs. Cutter's advice was very different from that of others back home, who felt an aging bachelor at twenty-five was somewhat of a nuisance. As I look back on it, my plans represented a contrast in opinion from east to west, culture to culture, and religion to religion. That contrast, of course, still exists. Many young people today believe they must finish school and establish themselves in their careers before starting a family. My own feelings were that I wanted to accomplish those goals *with* my wife. Many think this is antiquated thinking. I believed that achieving objectives *together* was part of the cement that would strengthen our marriage. It's still my conviction that accomplishing our achievements together accounts for a substantial part of my professional success and the success of our marriage and family.

Mary-Jo and I spent a lot of money during the fall of 1973 and the spring of 1974 on long-distance phone calls, she being at BYU in Utah and me being in Boston at Boston College.

Finally, after the semester was over, on May 14, 1974, we were married and sealed for eternity in the Salt Lake Temple in Utah.

After a wonderful honeymoon and extended visits with family and friends, I had some solid career decisions to make. Following graduation from Boston College with an MBA, my first inclination was to launch into political science, but I received advice from one of my professors, who felt I should instead move directly to Washington, D.C., study law at night, and get some firsthand experience on Capitol Hill.

I was accepted to The Potomac School of Law (now the George Mason University Law School). I also worked for six months in the Department of Agriculture and then was hired by the Clerk's Office of the U.S. House of Representatives. I felt obsessed with not wasting time. Though I was devoted to my wife and church assignments, I felt I had much positive professional work to do and only a limited amount of time to accomplish it.

Eventually, I worked for both Republicans and Democrats. In coming to Washington I had hoped to find the "only true political party," but I soon discovered that there was no such thing. I found conservative and liberal Democrats and Republicans. There were good Democrats and good Republicans, and in both parties there were clearly some who were not so good. It was often disappointing to observe firsthand the petty opposition and a striking inability to put personal feelings or party demands aside for a better cause. It became clear to me that people are people and we need to learn to work together in spite of our differences. Conflict itself appeared to be the nature of the process. I realized that it wasn't always bad to disagree. The important thing is how we treat each other.

I learned very swiftly that people could allow politics to take precedence over other things that are far more important. Nevertheless, at this time in my life I felt compelled by an urgency to prepare myself for a more active role. As Abraham Lincoln put it, "I think I've been bitten by the bug." To an outsider today, it might seem as if my decision to run for President of the United States is a little like shooting for the stars. And yet to those who know me well, this move into the political arena is a very natural course of events. The fact that I have not formerly been a senator or a congressman is an important point upon which I'll elaborate later in this book.

While I was exploring opportunities for more experience as an office manager or administrative assistant in a congressional office, I received numerous letters of reference in my behalf from congressmen. Frank Thompson, Jr. of New Jersey wrote: 'Dale has always been most competent in resolving any problems my office may have had in keeping up with the various accounts."

Mr. Gene Kennedy of Congresswoman Gladys Spellman's office was a person with whom I very much enjoyed working. He wrote the following in a letter of reference dated 16 February 1977: "In addition, his friendly demeanor, winning personality and superior knowledge he had of his field of responsibility make him an outstanding candidate . . . I have always found Mr. Christensen interested in the character and machinery of a Congressional office and he has shown intelligence and understanding of what should transpire in such an office. After seven years on Capitol Hill . . . I have determined that it is indeed rare to find someone with practical common sense as to what an office manager should be."

A few months later, I made the decision to work with Congressman Richard Tonry, a Democrat from the First District of Louisiana. It was my hope to watch and work with men of both parties so I could better judge for myself the appropriate party to which I would eventually become affiliated. With the job came turmoil and conflict. From the outset Mr. Tonry was plagued with political turbulence due to questions associated with the legality of his election. There were accusations that illegal money had passed hands, and that votes had been improperly counted. Nevertheless, I took the job as his office manager on May 1ˢᵗ, 1977. During the first few weeks, I took care of all of the Congressional business. Shortly after that, things quickly deteriorated for Mr. Tonry. He resigned to go home to Louisiana and run in a special election designed to establish a clear winner for his state's primary. In his absence, I was interviewed by several television and radio stations and appeared on the nightly news. Had Mr. Tonry prevailed in this re-election runoff, he would have returned to Washington, D.C. a hero. That was not the outcome. Because of activities that had taken place prior to my association with him, Tonry was indicted, tried, and found guilty of several crimes that sent him to prison for a year. However, because of the scandals surrounding Mr. Tonry, a Republican by the name of Robert Livingston finally won the seat—the first Republican from the state of Louisiana since the Civil War.

After this experience as office manager/fill-in Congressman, I clerked for the Dolan & Treanor law firm in Arlington, Virginia. While I was there I had the opportunity of working on several high-profile and very interesting cases, but I finally left with the impression that the practice of law was not for me. Instead, I needed to become directly involved with a political campaign. This turned out to be helping Ken Henderson try to win a seat as a U.S. Senator for the state of Kansas.

MaryJo and I attended the Republican campaign seminar in Denver, where I convinced Ken to run as a Republican instead of an independent. Immediately following his announcement, Ken received support from many of the farming and political organizations in Kansas. In 1978, there were multiple Republicans vying to fill a seat being vacated by outgoing Senator James Pearson. It was quickly evident that Nancy Landon Kassebaum, the only woman in the campaign, was receiving more publicity and support. Her father, Alf Landon, was a former governor of Kansas and had been a candidate for the United States presidency against Franklin D. Roosevelt in 1936. She went on to win the general election in November and became the first woman to be directly voted into the Senate without first serving in the House of Representatives.

It was an exhausting campaign, but tremendously important in my personal political understanding and conviction. I felt we had done all that we could do in that campaign. I came to see it as a genuine effort to preserve and defend American liberties, and I worked hard to develop a campaign platform around those themes. Even though we did not win, my wife and I, as well as many campaign staffers, felt that miracles had taken place in our personal lives, none more so than in mine. I came to see it as revelatory in my lifelong aspirations to preserve and defend American liberties. In working passionately to assist my candidate to develop a sound campaign platform, which he only partially accepted, I felt the most significant benefit was to my own mind and spirit.

It's important to note that many of the same themes I felt we were fighting for *then* are the same rights and freedoms I continue to fight for today—only now with an unprecedented fervor and urgency. Unless we can turn the tide threatening our Constitutional government, rights and freedoms, those very principles could be lost forever.

Chapter 6

The Seeds of Success

WHERE TO FIND OUR TREASURE

After the Kansas election, Mary-Jo and I returned to Connecticut for a well-deserved rest. I was concerned about our immediate future and devoted much thought and prayer to the matter. We had made plans to visit with my parents for a week or ten days in Idaho and travel through the Northwest, realizing it might be some time before we could do that again.

We enjoyed our trip very much, seeing the majestic sights of Idaho, Washington, Oregon and California. As we traveled through Utah I felt impressed to stop and call a friend, since we were just a few blocks away from his Salt Lake City office. When he found out where we were, he asked if I could come over and interview for a job with his company: Collier, Heinz and Associates. A short time later, I accepted their offer and worked as assistant vice president, and later as vice president of acquisitions in buying commercial shopping centers. This was the beginning of the next phase of my career as a businessman and entrepreneur.

My work required that I spend many, many late nights and sometimes sleep at the office, or just come home long enough to have dinner with Mary-Jo. When I did stay overnight, Mary-Jo came to be with me. Despite the lure of money and success and the thrill of the entrepreneurial game, in retrospect, I am convinced that regardless of how important any job is, it is never more important than spending time with your family.

In time, my salary was more than double what I was making before, and we purchased our first home, along with a new car and a second used one. The fruits of my labors were creating a comfortable life for us. However, we soon discovered that we were spending more than we were earning. Determined to avoid debt and financial bondage, we traded our two cars for a cheaper vehicle and sold the house to free ourselves so we could start to save money.

FIRST SOLO ACQUISITION

The first few months in my new job in acquisitions was very intensive and busy. We needed to acquire four shopping centers before year end. At the beginning of December, we had closed on three, but desperately needed one more. The morning of our company Christmas party, I was sent to Phoenix to put the Alta Vista shopping Center under contract. It was my first solo acquisition. My instructions were to boldly give the terms of our offer and walk out if not accepted.

The owner's Royles Royce was in his office driveway and Mr. Rubenstein wore a dark grey tux with patent leather shoes and stripes down his pants. He was a seasoned and successful business man who politely invited me to make my presentation. I did exactly as I'd been instructed and then used the foyer phone to call the home office for further instructions. I was told to go back, open my briefcase and present him with the written offer. If he did not accept it, I was to close my briefcase, walk out and fly home. He looked it over, laughed and tossed it back to me while saying that I was wasting my time and his. I did what I'd been told.

Just outside the door, I stopped and thought, "This is foolish! It is a terrible waste and we were not accomplishing anything." Determined, I opened up his office door and said, "Mr. Rubenstein, could we talk? I've never purchased a shopping center by myself before, but I think we can make a deal. Are you willing to go over the contract together?" He laughed and said, "No kidding! Come on over here." He arranged a chair on his side of the desk next to his. We went over the contract, point by point and traded price, payment hard costs, financing terms etc. When we finished, we both agreed that each of us ended up with more than we had hoped for so we made the changes and initialed them and signed the contract, shook hands and said goodbye. I had no time to call the office with the good news.

I returned in a blizzard with a signed contract and went straight to the party. As I walked in, everyone welcomed me home with encouraging comments like, "Better luck next time" and "We can't win them all". My boss put his arm around me, called for everyone's attention and proceeded to tell everyone what he thought had happened. When he was finished, I pulled the contact out of my suit pocket and showed him the signature page. His jaw dropped and he gasped as he contemplated the terms of the agreement. I felt like a hero.

OUR FAMILY EXPANDS

MaryJo and I had been married for six years. In spite of our prayers and efforts and a battery of tests by various doctors, we had not yet been able to have children. We had tried every recommendation. On occasion we would weep together as a couple, especially when well-meaning friends suggested we might be deliberately postponing this yearned-for opportunity. In time, we began to focus our energies toward the idea of adopting.

On October 10, 1979, Sister Simpson from LDS Social Services called me at my office and said, "I've been trying to get in touch with your wife all day."

"She's right here." I responded.

"Put her on," said Sister Simpson.

"She can hear you." I said. "We're on a speaker phone."

"Brother and Sister Christensen, I've got some news for you."

"Is it good news?" asked Mary-Jo. Later, she told me her whole body felt like it was on fire.

"I hope so." said Sister Simpson, "We've got a little girl for you, and you can come down and pick her up!"

We were dumfounded. "Right now?"

"Yes, but don't get into an accident on the way."

We were completely overcome. I ran out of my office yelling, "We have a baby!" Mary-Jo fell to her knees and couldn't stop sobbing. At the Social Services office, we were told that the baby had come a little premature, but she was healthy and doing well. We were led into a room where she was sleeping. Mrs. Simpson said, "I'll leave you alone with her for a few minutes."

There was our little daughter, all dressed in a pink outfit and a pink bow in her hair. She was a little doll, a tiny angel, a little princess.

While driving to the social service office, we sought a name for our child. All of a sudden, Mary-Jo knew it should be Teresa Joy. As only a parent can imagine, our new daughter had surpassed all our expectations. That night I awoke and saw MaryJo changing the baby's diaper.

"Is she wet?"

"No." said MaryJo.

"Then why are you changing her diaper?"

"I'm just practicing." she replied.

We sent an announcement to all our family and friends with the following description:

THE CHRISTENSEN NEW-BABY MODEL SHOWROOM

Proudly Announces the New 1979 Christensen Baby Model

Dale Christensen:
Owner and General Manager.

MaryJo Christensen:
Co-owner and Chief Maintenance Operator.

Model on display October 1979 has the following features: Two-lung power, free-squealing, scream-lined body, double-bawl bearing, water cooled exhaust, and changeable seat covers.

The management is happy to assure the public that there are no duplicate models available anywhere and that this original will be known as:

The 1979 Teresa Joy Model

Soon we experienced another miracle in our lives. We learned that our next child was to be born in midMay. Our dear friends, Kevin and Pam Rarick, who knew the birth mother, had recommended that we should be the parents. Immediately upon hanging up the phone I told MaryJo it would be a boy, and that I also knew his name. She said she did, too. We counted to three and both said "Samuel" at the same time.

In May we received the news announcing Samuel's birth. I was in New Orleans on business at the time. Mary-Jo wrote, "I'm thrilled about the arrival of Samuel Christensen! Joy filled my whole body! I'm so awake and I can hardly contain myself! My first impulse was to call Dale."

"It's a boy!" Mary-Jo shouted into the phone.

"I'll be on the plane in twenty minutes!" I replied. We met at the hospital in California and brought him home together.

On Sunday, June 1, 1980, we went to church in Blackfoot, Idaho, where we officially named Teresa-Joy and gave her a father's blessing after her adoption had been finalized. Then I held Samuel up high and introduced our new son to the congregation. Everyone was so excited. Then I made another surprise announcement. I informed everyone that my Mary-Jo was pregnant.

I told the congregation, "We've had six years of famine in our marriage, without any children. We are now due for six years of plenty. At this rate, with one baby every seven months or three every year, in the next six years we should have about eighteen!" Everyone laughed and some applauded.

Mary-Jo was very busy taking care of two new babies. We named our second son Jonathan.

INTERNATIONAL BUSINESS TRAVEL

At this particular time, my career focus was to sell shopping centers to foreign investors. Instead of going through middlemen, I was determined to find the investors directly. I planned a trip to visit people with whom I had been corresponding in numerous countries around the world. I asked my father if he would accompany me as my traveling companion.

We left Salt Lake City in January, 1982, for Hawaii and New Zealand. We went on to Sydney and Perth, Australia, before stopping in Japan, Korea, and Hong Kong. We had to pass over India on our way to Bahrain, Cairo, Tel Aviv, and Jerusalem. We stopped and spent time in Athens and Rome. While in Rome, my briefcase was stolen, along with our passports, tickets, and business information. We got everything worked out, but had to return directly home, bypassing Germany, France, and Great Britain. If the Internet had been available, we could have continued our business trip, but in 1982 this wasn't possible. I would have to return another time.

While traveling though the South Pacific and Asia we attended church meetings on several U.S. military bases. I wrote home saying, "I am so grateful, and my heart was filled with love for all the sacrifices made, and those willing to be made, in my behalf." I expressed this same gratitude directly to soldiers who were serving and realized how much we all take for granted living in the United States of America. More than ever my love of this country soared with the awe I felt toward those who have made America what it is today in goodness and greatness.

VIVA MEXICO!

Later, while on vacation in Mazatlán, Mary-Jo said she would like to see Mexico City and Guadalajara. For some time,

I'd had a growing desire to study and obtain a doctorate in International Relations and Political Science. We extended our trip for a few more days, visiting Guadalajara and Puerto Vallarta on our way back to Mazatlán.

I knew there was a lot of money coming into the United States from Mexico, but while doing business in Utah we'd never been able to have direct contact with the actual buyers. Soon after returning home we made an extraordinary decision as a family—we would move to Mexico. I decided to go to Mexico with my brother and find business buyers. Mary-Jo stayed behind to liquidate everything we owned and prepare our family to make the move. I returned to finalize the sale of our house and to complete the biggest garage sale Utah had ever seen. We sold our brand new car and drove to Mexico in a 1969 Ford LTD that we'd purchased from my parents for $10.

We settled our family in a neighborhood of Mexico City, apartment #3, 146 Empresa in Mixcoac. We shopped each day for fresh fruits, vegetables and breads and "pollo al brazo" for dinner. We also learned to love the food of the Mexican street vendors. For many foreigners, this food was infamous for causing gastrointestinal problems. For some reason my family never got sick from these foods, and we never worried about such problems. We tried everything and learned to deeply love the culture, the people, and everything Mexican. Mary-Jo and I immersed ourselves in our Spanish classes and studied diligently to master the Spanish language.

It was my misfortune, however, that at this particular time the economy in Mexico was weak and suddenly took a dramatic turn for the worse. In 1982 the peso had plunged in value from 22 pesos per American dollar in February, to 45 pesos in March, to 110 pesos per dollar in August. Sure, it was great for Americans with dollars to live there, but not for

Mexicans. Money was leaving the country at a record clip. The situation had become grave for Mexican citizens.

At the end of August, circumstances were dire, and there was a growing fear of unrest. The President of Mexico was going to speak to the whole nation. We were advised not to go out of our houses on August 31 or all day on September 1st. The emotions we felt and the suspense we endured were the same as anyone else living in Mexico. I'd just risked a lot of money and invested a lot of time and effort to make our family's home and business in this beautiful place. The day arrived, and we watched television with great anticipation as the President of Mexico delivered his national broadcast. My Spanish wasn't particularly good at this time, but I told Mary-Jo that it sounded to me like the president was going to nationalize the banks. He described what was happening and gave a lot of reasons for what needed to be done. Finally he announced the nationalization of all Mexican banks. For Mexicans it was suddenly illegal to take their capital out of the country to buy properties in the United States. I was shocked. I was suddenly out of a job.

We made plans for the necessary changes this would bring. We stayed for another month just to enjoy the beautiful sights of Mexico and improve our Spanish. At last we returned to the United States, and I prepared to embark on a new career adventure and reinvent myself yet again.

In January of 1983, I began to apply for graduate schools to obtain a doctorate in Public Administration or Political Science. I applied to ten schools, with an objective to develop my professional skills. I also began to take an advanced Spanish language class with the U.S. Department of Agriculture.

Then, on Friday, February 11, we received a call from LDS Church Headquarters in Salt Lake City. We were so excited that I almost pulled the phone off the wall. The call was from Elder L. Tom Perry's secretary. Elder Perry, my former stake president in Boston, was now a member of the Quorum of the Twelve Apostles of The Church of Jesus Christ of Latter-day Saints. He wanted to set up a screening interview with me as a possible candidate to serve as a mission president. His secretary asked me to bring my wife and made it clear that the interview was not an official call. It was just a preliminary interview to assess the *likelihood* of a call in the future. At the interview we informed Elder Perry of our desire to serve and told him that we were ready to go in a moment's notice. He told us that nothing would take place immediately, but asked us not to make any commitments that would extend longer than a year.

A mission president in the LDS Church is someone who leads and "fathers" all those Sunday-dressed young men and young women with black name tags who are called by a prophet of God to be representatives for the Lord Jesus Christ. The missionaries travel through neighborhoods of the world on foot or on bicycles, or sometimes in mission automobiles. In those days a mission president and his wife (this calling required just as much responsibility and commitment from a wife) might preside over as many as 250 young men, young women, and mature retired married couples.

TAMARA DAWN

Just before we left Mexico, we had learned that we were about to become parents for the fourth time. Mary-Jo was a low-risk expectant mother and had a very comfortable and healthy pregnancy with Jonathan. This time we were going to try something new when it came time to deliver our baby. She would be delivered at home by a midwife.

On June 3 of 1983 Tamara Dawn became the newest member of the family and tenant of our townhouse apartment in Waldorf, Maryland. The morning of her birth, the sun was streaming through the bedroom window. For me it was a glorious moment. I went to the front window and shouted to the children outside that it was a baby girl. Mary-Jo's mother had been waiting just beyond the bedroom/delivery room door. Teresa Joy, Samuel, and Jonathan entered the bedroom one by one to meet and bond with their new baby sister.

THE CALL

Late one evening in December 1983, the telephone rang. We were greeted by the voice of President Gordon B. Hinckley, a member of the First Presidency of The Church of Jesus Christ of Latter-day Saints. He later served as the President of the church from 1995 to 2008. He asked if he could take some time, and then conducted an interview with me over the phone. After an interview that confirmed my desire and spiritual worthiness, he asked if we had children and how old they were. I answered, "Yes, we have four, and they are one, two, three, and four years old."

He repeated the question and I repeated my answer.

He must have been teasing because he said, "Are you planning on taking them with you?" I wanted to tease him right back and say, "Well, we'd planned to take them with us—unless you and Sister Hinckley could help babysit them for us for a while." but I didn't think it was appropriate.

His tone became serious and he said, "Brother Christensen, you can consider this interview an official call from the Lord to serve as mission president in an English or Spanish-speaking mission. You will receive your assignment next spring, and we would ask that you don't discuss this with anyone until your call is officially announced." I accepted the call and assured him that we would follow his instructions.

We would be living in the mission home, with a mission vehicle. Most of the mission travel and missionary food expenses would be taken covered. Our expenses wouldn't be excessive.

We left Maryland at the end of March so we could attend General Conference in Salt Lake City, Utah, and to visit with our family and friends in Utah and Idaho until we left for the mission field. At that time there were hundreds of countries and various parts of the world that had been divided up into specific mission areas. Mary-Jo and I had felt personally impressed that we would be serving in a Spanish-speaking area.

Finally, we were told the answer to the question that had kept us on pins and needles. We were overjoyed to learn that our mission assignment was to serve in the Peru Lima South Mission. It felt right, and it felt like home. I immediately immersed myself in everything I could learn about the country, the people, their customs, and the history of the LDS Church in that part of the world.

I was set apart as mission president by Elder Dallin H. Oaks, a member of the Quorum of the Twelve Apostles. Mary-Jo was also set apart as my missionary companion and an official church representative. Elder Oaks blessed me that I would have the protecting care of Heavenly Father and promised that angels would watch over me and shield my family if .I acted with faith and prayer while observing common sense and necessary precautions. At this time, Peru was experiencing serious problems with terrorism, along with economic and social unrest.

Of course, if serious political unrest had ever erupted during my three-year tenure, it would have been my job to gather up all the missionaries under my supervision, get them to a place of protection, and, if necessary, shepherd them out of the country. In the meantime, our work as missionaries was not to worry about politics. Our work was to build up the spiritual—and temporal—welfare of the local Latter-day Saints and bless the lives of every citizen of Peru. We did this in multiple ways including teaching about Jesus Christ and service projects designed to improve the living conditions for the people. We strived to increase hygiene and standards of living in both the cities and in the countryside, as well as help people deal with every imaginable kind of physical and emotional distress. The most basic definition of a missionary for The Church of Jesus Christ of Latter-day Saints is simply to be a representative of the Savior and servant of the people in whatever capacity he or she might be called upon to perform.

MISIÓN PERÚ LIMA SUR

We arrived in Lima shortly after midnight on June 30, 1984. When we arrived, we had 232 missionaries, about 85 percent North American and 15 percent Peruvian. Among these were three senior married couples. There were 3,354 members of the church organized into 15 branches (smaller congregations) inside our mission boundaries. In time, the average number of missionaries grew to 286, with only 15 percent North American and 85 percent Peruvian. When we left, there were over 11,000 members in 59 branches and 9 districts. However, while we were there the three Peruvian missions were subdivided to form a fourth. In summary, our missionaries baptized over 14,000 new members of the church as well as achieved great success in countless other humanitarian projects and spiritual efforts.

This was an unforgettable experience—to live in an entirely different culture with new vistas, climates and terrain. As with

Mexico, we learned to love the people in a way that many Americans who've never lived abroad might find difficult to understand and appreciate. We lived at sea level and drove over the 19,000-foot-high Ticlio mountain pass to get to the Altiplano and again over the eastern passes to wind our way down to the dry jungle through La Merced to Pozuso and Satipo and then on to the lush green rainforest beyond Cuzco and Macchu Picchu to Madre de Dios, a town at the headwaters of the Amazon River. We traveled up and down the coast of Peru, which encompasses some of the driest deserts in the world. However, wherever water was brought out of the mountains for irrigation, the country was indescribably fertile and green.

We witnessed the construction of the new Lima Peru LDS Temple and participate in its dedicatory services. Temples represent the pinnacle in LDS worship, which is centered on Jesus Christ. Prior to the construction of a temple in Lima, LDS members had to travel all the way to Santiago, Chile, or Sao Paulo, Brazil, in order participate in temple worship. As construction began, Mary-Jo and I were invited to apply some of the mortar in placing the cornerstone.

At first only local missionaries serving in Lima were invited to attend the temple dedication. This left out missionaries serving in other parts of the mission, perhaps because of concerns over inconvenience, expense, or their safety. I was concerned that many missionaries would never have another chance to witness such an event. I shared this perspective with one of the bodyguards attending to church President Gordon B. Hinckley, who had arrived in Lima for the dedicatory service. The very next day, President Hinckley asked all the mission presidents, "All the missionaries are going to attend, aren't they?" His meaning was clear. All missionaries were invited to make their way to Lima for this sacred event.

In a letter to me on February 5, 1986, President Gordon B. Hinckley wrote:

"Thank you for your handwritten note . . . expressing appreciation in behalf of your missionaries to attend the Lima Peru Temple dedication and also the missionary meeting which we held Sunday evening. My only regret is that all of the missionaries in that area were not advised earlier. Most of them really will never have an opportunity to attend a temple dedication and I am very glad that things worked out as they did, even though the notice was short. It was a pleasure to see you and Sister Christensen. I am confident that you are having a wonderful time, and I know that you are doing great work. Our prayers are with you."

Sister Dodi Westwood shared with me what she wrote in her missionary journal dated Saturday, March 1, 1986.

"President Christensen spoke to us today . . . as I watched him . . . I felt deep within my heart his divine calling. He loves Peru and each one of his missionaries. I have rarely seen a love so deep and so unconditional in men. . . . He truly does love us for who we are and who we can become—no matter how great the difference may be between the two. I will never forget the look on his face or the tears in his eyes today, nor the spirit that rests upon him and is felt by those around him. He . . . has the kind of love that Christ taught—charity—the pure love of Christ. I pray that I, too, may be able to develop this love which touches people's lives so profoundly."

I appreciated her heartfelt sentiment and only hope that I can make her description accurate and be as she saw me. One might wonder what such characteristics might have to do with a future President of the United States. My reply is that faith and spiritual strength should be considered *paramount* attributes for any leader of any country. We must acknowledge that something higher than ourselves helps to direct the "affairs of men" and is also available to assist those who are granted the opportunity to serve their fellow men. In short, it keeps a leader humble and diligent in the office in which he serves. Such a leader recognizes and honors the reality that a Higher Authority is truly in charge and that we are merely His stewards. In my view, we do not want or need leaders who are obsessed with the laurels or accolades that position and power might bring. Instead, we want and need leaders who are concerned with the welfare of those they serve and the judgment of God regarding how leaders treat others with the authority and trust given them.

TERRORISM

During our time in Peru, we had a constant threat of terrorism. There were frightening incidents that forced us to our knees. On several occasions we had to turn to the military for help. Once a bus with our missionaries as passengers was attacked high on a mountain pass by members of the "Shining Path," a terror organization. Armed soldiers were traveling with the bus to protect it. None of our missionaries were hurt in the incident, but they told me that after the attack was over, they had to jump over dead bodies as they raced back to board the bus and continue on their journey. During similar encounters in many areas of the country, innocent people were killed.

On another occasion, a remote village high in the Andes Mountains was attacked. A local LDS branch leader told the members of his congregation that they needed to evacuate immediately. Nine families followed him, bypassing terrorist positions without being noticed and remaining hidden in a distant field for many hours. An hour after midnight, everyone in the village was killed and all their possessions were taken, but those who had followed their church leader survived.

A year later, I sent to this village a member of our mission presidency and a missionary to take the members some pots and pans, cooking utensils, clothing, and some money for food. The members had almost nothing and were living in the fields. On their way, my envoy was stopped by a group of terrorists and searched. For a while, the missionaries thought they were going to be killed, but convinced the terrorists that they were all brothers and sisters just trying to help those in need. They were freed, but I didn't feel that it was safe to send anybody back.

Shortly after I left Peru, two missionaries were killed in *Huancayo*. All missionaries and mission leadership from North American were evacuated. Some top LDS leaders, including a mission president who followed me, had been placed upon Shining Path hit lists. They were forced to drive their vehicles directly onto the tarmac of the Lima airport and board their scheduled flight out of the country. Years later, these political problems were resolved, and some of the contingent of North American missionaries returned, side by side with Peruvians, and continued their work serving the people of Peru.

I thank God for the opportunity to immerse myself in another culture. To this day I have such intense feelings of love for the people of Peru that I can hardly contain my emotions as I think about it. These are among my most cherished memories.

Chapter 7

Pathway to Destiny

RETURN WITH HONOR

We returned home from Peru to a wonderful homecoming with our family and friends in Idaho Falls, Idaho. We were so happy to be home in the United States. We spent time visiting friends and family in Idaho, Utah, and California. Then we began work developing and selling shopping centers in Salt Lake City and a hospital in Las Vegas. In celebration of our return to the States, every member of the family got new cowboy boots, hats, and traditional Western clothes. We went to the parade and rodeo in Blackfoot, Idaho, where we celebrated the 4th of July. Oh, to be back in America! We relished the fireworks, ice-cream, chili, hot dogs, swimming, and go-cart rides. The highlight was pledging allegiance to the flag and singing the national anthem with fellow Americans. The next day we celebrated my thirty-ninth birthday.

My family had lived in Peru for three long years. For children, three years can seem like a lifetime. Clearly my children had come to recognize a lot of differences between Peru and the United States. Coming home presented some interesting and challenging adjustments. Also, we had to move back into our home in Centerville, Utah. We had sold it years earlier, but the people we'd sold it to let it fall back into our hands. They had built a new house and couldn't make both payments.

As one of our first financial ventures upon returning home, I made a sizeable investment in raising green peppers in Baja California, Mexico, with someone we met in Peru. Our whole family went there to see the operation. Everything seemed to be pointing to success. It was an exciting adventure, but the weather was unusually cold, and our crop was late getting to the Los Angeles marketplace. We lost all our capital and never recouped any of it. Mary-Jo had seen this from the beginning. She said, "The profit might be there, but whether we'll ever realize it is another thing. Why am I so skeptical? I hope I eat my words." Instead, her skepticism proved prophetic.

Again in 1987, I felt the same political aspirations that I'd felt ever since my mother had told me I could one day run for President. On October 8, 1987, the *Deseret News* in Salt Lake City announced that I was going to run for Congress against Utah Congressman Wayne Owens. We were interviewed on television, and for a brief moment this seemed the opportune time to pursue this ambition. However, Mary-Jo was very reluctant. Several other friends and associates whom I respected counseled me not to run. I followed their advice to work in commercial real estate for the time being and pursue politics at some future time. Nevertheless, throughout my life I've felt I had something very positive to offer in the world of politics. I've felt a strong obligation to become involved and to serve. Now, in this upcoming 2016 election, that time is finally here.

In 1987 my family and I had written down certain goals we wanted to achieve. I felt I should pursue these goals before jumping into the political arena. One objective was to purchase 1,000 acres of farmland. We decided to look first in Utah, then Connecticut or New York, and finally in Idaho.

Months later, without even knowing our family had this goal, our dear neighbor, Andy Bavelas, came over to my house carrying a newspaper that contained a classified ad listing an Amish farm for sale in Missouri. When I looked at the advertised price and number of acres, I said with excitement, "Andy, we can do this. I'll buy half and you buy half!" I called my brother-in-law, Mike Kelsey, and the next day he and his son Jed, Andy Bavelas, and my son Samuel, and I went to Missouri to buy the farm.

After seeing the property, the realtor asked if we would like to see any other farms that were selling in the area. She showed us many different properties that caught my eye. We finally bought 220 acres in Coffey, Missouri. I also wanted to purchase the 690-acre McKinsey farm in Jameson, but it wasn't for sale. I gave the current owners my card and asked them to call me if they ever decided to sell. Within six months, I purchased the McKinsey farm at an auction on the court house steps. We later purchased the Gwinn Farm and the Corbin Farm, for a total of almost 1,500 acres. We had met our written goal. We later sold some parcels to pay off the mortgage on the McKinsey parcel, my favorite of the three properties.

FRANKLIN QUEST COMPANY

On April 17, 1989, I began working with the Franklin Quest Company. At the time, Franklin was the largest time-management education company in the world. They later merged with Stephen R. Covey's Leadership Center to become Franklin Covey. I was trained and worked in the Salt Lake City office for a time, but was one of the first two representatives to move out into the field. We sold our home in Utah, filled up a 24-foot U-Haul, and moved to Connecticut. As we traveled across country I had each one of the children with me in the truck to have one-on-one time with Daddy. Each one talked about everything, sharing their hopes and dreams. The rest of the family followed in a Voyager minivan.

Six months after moving into our neighborhood in Connecticut, I was called to be the bishop of our local church congregation, known as a ward. Immediately following the meeting, someone tapped me on the shoulder and told me I had my first funeral to conduct. An elderly member in the ward had just passed away that day. I hadn't even had an opportunity to meet that person.

CHRISTENSEN FAMILY CONSTITUTION, SHERMAN, CONNECTICUT, 1989

On Christmas Day, I announced that we would hold a family council and write a family constitution to establish our family's values and goals. Five-year-old Tamara empathically said, "Oh no, that means we have to fight a war!"

I said, "No Tamara, the fighting is over. Now it's time to write our own constitution just like our Founding Fathers did for our country." I asked what they wanted, and Mary-Jo and I wrote down what everyone said. After several hours of brainstorming, negotiating, and redrafting, the following draft of our own family constitution was ratified during our next Monday night Family Home Evening:

1. **We are a Christ-centered family**. We focus on individual and family spiritual welfare as the most important aspect of being an eternal family. We are disciples of Christ, and we follow Him. We learn of Him, speak of Him, worship the Father through Him and try to be like Him.

2. **We are a united family**. We love one another and put our family ahead of other things. We always support each other and want to be together and do things together. We are different and unique in a very special way.

3. **We are a good family**. We are nice, kind, sweet, and courteous. We are a serving, helpful, caring family. We do for others what they cannot do for themselves. We are a sharing and giving family and love others. We are a missionary family and strive to be a good example to others.

4. **We are a well-rounded family**. We are wise stewards in managing our time, talents, resources, and assets. We are happy and fun loving. We are intelligent and stimulating and always seeking for truth and we value knowledge and learning. We continually explore all of God's creations and man's inventions. We are healthy and active. We are neat and orderly. We are international, cosmopolitan, hometown, and country.

5. **We are a patriotic family**. We love freedom and obey the law. We respect the rights, property and ideas of others. We are well-informed of current events, historical facts, and future prophesies. We are active in the political process and strive to defend freedom and justice.

6. **We are a prosperous family**. We are financially independent. We are free of debt and own our own home, land, and precious possessions. We work together to save and invest for the future. We are self-sufficient and prepare for disaster with home storage, insurance, investments, assets and estate planning.

A SACRED PASSING

1990 was turning out to be a very good year for the Christensen family. We felt highly blessed that our business

111

representing Franklin Quest was increasing at a healthy pace. It appeared that we would soon reach our goals, be debt free, pay off our farm, etc. We felt a good spirit in our home and knew that all of our children were happy, healthy and progressing. However, in October we experienced a tender event.

On October 12, 1990, my father, Irven Christensen, passed away at the age of 90. He had been uncomfortable for quite some time after prostrate surgery and afterwards developed an obstructed intestine. Over a six-month period he lost substantial weight. At the time of his death, he had 10 children, 50 grandchildren, and 64 great grandchildren. We flew our whole family to Idaho for the funeral.

On October 13, 1990 Mary-Jo wrote: "Our family flew to Salt Lake City this morning. Yesterday, I think I was on a walk talking to an old man when Dad died. Our sister-in-law, Leslie, called to let me know. Dale was gone to an appointment in New York City so I called and told him. He asked my advice about what we should do about going to the funeral. Dad probably would have told us not to come. We decided (with a stupor of thought) that just Dale would go. I decided to tell the children that this was the plan. I announced to them, 'Something very special has happened to Grandpa Christensen.' They didn't quite comprehend, so I reworded it, 'Something happy for him, but sad for us.' Then they knew and were very upset.

"Samuel wanted to go to the wedding (which we explained would be a funeral), but I told him that only Daddy was going and that we'd already purchased non-changeable/non-refundable tickets for November, when the whole family would be going. Samuel insisted that he had to see his Grandpa one more time before we all meet him again in heaven. I didn't realize that going to the funeral would mean so much to him. So I said that if we could get our tickets refunded I would ask

Dad. The airline said yes. I no longer had a stupor of thought. We knew that our whole family making the journey was the right thing to do.

"By the time Dale got home from New York, it was 10 p.m. After a discussion, he agreed that the whole family should fly to Idaho. At that late hour, I began to prepare for our plane trip. We had to leave our house at 10:30 a.m. and we had to pack everything necessary for a family of six. We also had to make arrangements for the house, the pets, and take care of business for the week we would be gone."

Mary-Jo and I packed and got ready for the long trip. A small miracle happened at the airport. The girl at the desk noticed that we had "compassion-priced" tickets and only charged us $78 instead of $275-$300 for each ticket. This saved us over $1,800.

Just weeks earlier my father had said to my brother Karl, "I'm such a burden to your mother."

My mother told my father, "Irven, you can go."

Dad didn't want to leave Mother alone. In a world where people feel bad about themselves, are hard on themselves and down on themselves, and so negative, Dad was always accepting and uplifting. No matter who you were he would make you feel good. He was supportive of everything we did—where we moved and even the dumb decisions we often made. He remembered everything about everyone and asked you about every single person. There's no person we knew who'd ever treated people nicer. He would visit with everyone at any occasion and prevent anyone from leaving before he had a chance to visit with them.

My father was a man without guile. At the funeral, my father's bishop in Blackfoot, Idaho, said, "His last public testimony at church was given from the pulpit after he slowly walked to the front with the aid of his walker and said, 'I just want you to know whose side I am on!'" He meant the Lord's side, and he expressed that he was willing to trade houses with the bishop's family with all five of his children. "The bishop had a small house, he said, and we had a large one." The next day, he had the bowel obstruction requiring surgery. While he was in the hospital, he told my mother about seeing people from the other side of the veil in his room.

The viewing was before the funeral service. I felt I was a little irreverent at the viewing because I was visiting with all of the family members that I hadn't seen for quite a while, but as I think about it, that's how my father would have wanted it.

During my funeral remarks, I told about an agreement my father and my Uncle Jeff Davis had made with each other that they would speak at each other's funeral. I explained that when Uncle Jeff passed away, father had spoken at his funeral. So, just then, I played a recording of Uncle Jeff's voice while giving a sermon. I told the audience, "I'm sure they are both having a good laugh about this right now." The congregation erupted in laughter.

The service itself was wonderful—such a tribute to Dad. The chapel and cultural hall were filled to overflowing, and even in the seats behind the podium, generally occupied by the choir. People were crammed as tightly as sardines. Dad obviously had a lot of people who loved him.

BILL CLINTON DREAM

Idaho and Utah were predominantly Republican. Most of my family did not like Democratic President Bill Clinton's politics or behavior. I disagreed with him on many issues, but I regularly and sincerely prayed for him.

One night I had a dream about him. The dream struck me as very interesting—so much so that it inspired me to write to him the following letter on November 14, 1996:

Dear President Clinton,

My family and I recently moved to Utah from Connecticut. While I am a registered Republican and politically differ with you in many ways, I have recently had two experiences that have dramatically changed my feelings toward you as a person:

1. During a political meeting I found myself looking over all the books, literature, buttons and other campaign paraphernalia laid out on the long row of tables in the lobby. I stopped at one table when I noticed several rolls of toilet paper with your picture on it. One of the men behind the table asked me with gusto, "What axe do you want to grind?" When I told him I didn't have an axe to grind, he chided back, "Come on, you're not doing any good unless you have something to bash!" Somewhat dismayed, I said, "Listen Mister, I'm not a Democrat. I didn't vote for Clinton and I don't like a lot of his thinking, but he is the President of the United States! He's my president and I'm offended that you would put his picture on toilet paper and display it this way. You ought to be ashamed of yourself!" I just walked away feeling put off by what this man was doing.

2. After campaigning very hard and voting against you, I was disappointed that my candidate did not win. However, last night I had a dream about you. In my dream we met on a large lawn by the White House and we spoke personally while we walked on a wide path connecting two large beautiful homes. Even more significant than our conversation was the overwhelming feeling that filled me as we said good-bye, and you continued on to meet with many others. Perhaps this dream was just for my benefit, but when I woke up and told my wife about it, I decided to also share these things with you. Thank you for conducting yourself the way you did during the campaign. Our family has just knelt in prayer to ask God to bless you and all the other elected officials to be wise, good, and honest as you work together or in opposition to one another within the framework of our Constitution in helping to protect and maintain individual rights and liberties. This is paramount over the economy, social benefits or our position in the world. May God bless you in your task.

Sincerely, Dale Christensen

Ever since that night, I've looked forward to the time when we could meet in person—face to face—and talk in private. It is my desire to exceed his expectations in all aspects of life. For example, during each of the last five years at Franklin Quest Co., I was one of the top five producers among their 120-125 sales executives. Now, more than ever, I strive to excel in ways that are not measured monetarily.

CHINA

From 1998 and 1999, I'd worked as president of a startup company selling a construction product to China. Our company was called The Great Wall New Building System. I'd traveled back and forth many times, staying for a few weeks or two months. We were finally purchased by a group out of New York City and Florida.

I continued to work for this company, fully expecting an announcement at any day that we would pick up and move to China. Mary-Jo and I were ecstatic about the idea of living in the Far East and began seeking permanent housing to establish our permanent headquarters there. The new owners, however, decided they wanted our headquarters to stay in the U.S. They also wanted me to renegotiate our contracts with our Chinese partners. I felt very uncomfortable working under these parameters. In my heart, I knew I couldn't do this after promising the Chinese that we would be good partners. I began looking for other business opportunities in China and was recruited by a Chinese university to be a professor in their MBA program.

It all happened during November 2000 when I helping to translate a UNESCO Research Project. I was asked to lecture to the MBA students at the University of Science & Technology of China (USTC) in the evenings for several days. The Chinese called this school their "MIT of China." It was where the country had developed its nuclear capabilities before moving these operations off campus. A gentleman approached me and said, "The students really like you. Would you consider being a professor at our university? We would like you to teach business classes in English." I accepted the offer and turned in my resignation to my company. My classes included Entrepreneurship, Business Communications, International Business and later Teaching Techniques for their Chinese professors.

For the next six months we traveled all over China and had interviews with CEOs and plant managers of large industrial factories about their awareness and opinions regarding environmental issues. I spoke in many cities in China. We were always treated with profound respect and hospitality. There were countless bicycles, umbrellas, layered clothing and different food, sounds, and smells. I personally watched a transformation taking place in the Chinese people and in their economy over the next three years. Since then, I've continued to observe from a distance I remain amazed at the progress they are making.

My speeches were generally about business and politics and the exploration of business opportunities between the United

States and China. During my travels, I became good friends with the mayor of Hefei City. During one dinner party, I told the mayor that if he trained his assistant well, perhaps when he became the Prime Minister of China, his assistant would replace him as mayor of Hefei. Well, he loved the idea and toasted me three times.

At this particular period, the U.S. was in the midst of its 2000 election challenges and the vote counts in Florida. The mayor asked me how we were going to solve the Bush-Gore problem and added, "Why don't you go and just tell them both you will be the President and solve it." I laughed and told him that it may be easier for him to become Prime Minister of China than for me to become the President of the United States, but if we both succeeded we would have a big celebration party and good relations would persist between our countries. He toasted me again and we shook hands.

A PROFESSOR IN CHINA

I traveled many times from Shanghai to Nanjing, Changzhou, Hangzhou, Wushi, Beijing and to Hefei, lecturing and teaching business and entrepreneurism. In January of 2000 I began teaching in the MBA program at the University of Science and Technology (USTI). During the previous months, I wrote the textbook for the entrepreneur class I was to teach. It was titled *The Entrepreneur's Guide: The Ultimate Learning and Business Experience*. Later, I wrote *10 Secrets to Speaking English*. Everyone seemed to want to improve their spoken English. Even though they had studied for many years, most were still afraid to speak. Our students were very kind to us and took us out to dinner so they could practice speaking English and for us to practice speaking Chinese. We tasted many delicious and exotic dishes, established lifelong friendships, and made many happy memories.

China is a beautiful country. The Chinese know much about the West, but westerners know little about China or the Chinese people.

There is an old Chinese saying that, "The five most beautiful mountains are in China. If you see them, you don't need to see any other mountains. The Yellow Mountain is the most beautiful mountain of them all. If you see the Yellow Mountain, you do not have to see any of the other four." We had a lovely trip to the Yellow Mountain. It really was a unique and spectacular experience and view. We then visited Tunxi, an ancient village dating back almost 1,000 years. We saw the most beautiful countryside, with rice paddies and tea bushes covering the hills and mountainsides. And of course, no one can visit China without seeing the ancient Chinese capital of Xian and the Terracotta Warriors. There were so many other historic and beautiful places we enjoyed visiting.

SUN MING

One of my most satisfying experiences in China was tutoring Sun Ming, my MBA student who had won a scholarship for a two-year master's degree in bank financing at Hong Kong University. Among thousands who took the examination to win the scholarship, she was one of the few who passed and was chosen for an interview. For months, we worked long and hard together to help prepare her for the interview. I was very proud of her and think she will be leading one of China's banks in the future. She was working fulltime in her bank and attending class in the Executive MBA program on weekends.

HONESTY AND INTEGRITY

At the end of one of our semesters, in June of 2001, I offered a final exam to my students. This exam consisted of three very easy questions and also three extra-credit questions.

I gave clear instructions about how to take the exam and instructed the students not to use notes. Nor were they allowed to help each other. The exam took considerably less time than had been allotted, and the scores came in much higher than I expected.

The problem came about as I saw two students cheating by looking in their notebooks for answers. Needless to say, I was surprised and disappointed that this could happen in my class, particularly with me walking up and down the aisles and carefully watching over the classroom during the exam period. After the exam and the class was dismissed, I asked the two students whom I'd witnessed cheating to come to my home that evening and discuss the final exam.

They came with two other classmates to help persuade me to let them pass and get credit for the exam. I had seen one looking at notes on the chair next to him and the other in a book on the windowsill. In the beginning they admitted to having cheated a little bit. They both confessed to having done what I saw. When we finished, they acknowledged their errors and one agreed to give a five-minute presentation on honesty and the other on integrity. I told them that they would not get credit for the exam, but I would consider how they might do some extra work to help their grades. In an effort to help them save face, I promised I would not say anything to any other student in the class.

Another interesting thing to me was why their two fellow students had come to our home at 10:00 p.m. at night in a heavy rainstorm after their last weekend class. They were concerned that I was offended and may not come back to teach the following year. They explained the culture of cheating in their schools and how they often dealt with dishonesty, even by their own friends. They insisted that close friends would tell them they were being a fool if they were honest or behaved with integrity because "everyone cheats." I was touched by their thoughtfulness and comments. They expressed appreciation that I would take the time to correct their behavior and teach them about honesty while some professors would turn their heads and ignore the cheating as though it was not happening.

At the beginning of the next class, these two students gave fine presentations on honesty and integrity to their fellow classmates. Just before their presentations, I'd taken them into the hall and reminded them that they did not need to verbally apologize. I had not mentioned their names and did not plan to. However, they both insisted on making an open apology. They also wrote riveting, humble letters of apology to me and to the class, stating things like, "I'm very sorry that my wrong behavior really hurt your heart. I apologize sincerely. Thank you so much for the lesson you taught me. I think this is my vital turning point to my successful life. I say thanks again to you, my dear teacher."

One wrote, "An honest person is one who aspires to follow the highest codes of conduct; is one who is loyal to the universal principles of life; whose decisions are based clearly on what is right and wrong; and one who does not misuse, abuse, or waste the wealth of resources."

The last student expressed a heartfelt apology to the class for dishonoring them. He said that this was the most important class of his life and had offered him the greatest lesson that he had ever learned. He expressed his appreciation for the chance to learn and then told about two famous American presidents. One was known for honesty and the other for a lack of integrity. He went on to speak about Abraham Lincoln and Bill Clinton. His personal idol was Jack Welch of General Electric. The student declared that if he didn't change his habits now, he would never be able to realize his goal of being the "Jack Welch of China." He promised "never to make the same mistake and to be honest forever from now on."

It wasn't my intention to come to China to teach ethics or morality. I had come to teach business and entrepreneurship. Nevertheless, I felt this experience was one of the most valuable teaching opportunities of my career. I hoped it would have a lasting effect upon the students who had placed themselves under my tutelage.

SEPTEMBER 11, 2001

While still living in China, we watched the CCTV news early in the morning following the terrorist attack on the twin towers of the World Trade Center in New York City. This affected us as deeply as any other American family, even though we were living on the other side of the globe. Our family prayed for the leaders of our nation and also for the leaders of other nations. We also prayed sincerely for our enemies and those who had destroyed so many lives. We prayed that their hearts would be softened. We also prayed that justice would be served and that further destruction and evil would be stopped.

America's legacy on that account, I believe, is mixed. Like other Americans, I felt proud of our men and women in uniform and those serving in other areas of national defense who brought justice to the doorstep of many terrorists, including those directly responsible for what happened in New York, Washington, D.C., and Pennsylvania. My concern was that we, as a nation, were becoming too closely entangled in the affairs of other nations to achieve that objective, often at too high a cost. I'll speak more about my positions with regard to foreign policy later in this book. Suffice it to say that despite my Constitutional feelings, I would be more reserved with regard to committing

American troops or resources to parts of the world that must pav their own way toward freedom and democracy.

2020 VISION SPEECH

In the fall of 2001, a woman came to my class and asked if I could translate a special invitation for the Anhui provincial government to host a series of meetings in Los Angeles, Chicago, and other cities. I was happy to do it. After helping her, the woman invited me to attend a special economic cooperation meeting at the Yellow Mountain the following week. During our conversation, I shared with her my idea about a United Nations City. She was really excited and wanted me to give a speech. I was not able to go at that time because of another commitment, so Mary-Jo agreed to represent me and give the speech on my behalf. I stayed up most of the night and early the next morning to finish the draft.

Mary-Jo spoke at the Anhui Provincial International Economic Cooperation Summit following Shanghai's APEC meetings at Huang Shan (Yellow Mountain). At that time, I was teaching a special two-day International Business course in Daqing and Harbin in northern China. Mary-Jo got to meet a lot of Chinese and foreign diplomats, business leaders and other dignitaries, including the United Nation's Director of Development. The speech appeared in local newspapers and other Chinese media. My students kept telling me that their families and the people of the community were truly excited about my idea to create a United Nations City in China. It was exciting to have such an opportunity to express these ideas and receive this kind of attention. We enjoyed the moment. Here are a few highlights from that speech:

Da Jiahao. My name is Mary-Jo Christensen, and I am a professor at the University of Science & Technology of China located in Hefei

City. As I frequently do, I am here representing Dale Christensen, my husband and business partner who was not able to be here because he had a previous engagement in Harbin in northern China. He is a visiting professor teaching in the business school and MBA program of USTC. We both love China with its delicious food, rich culture and history, but most of all, we love the Chinese people.

Dale sends his greetings, his apologies for not being here, and his best wishes to everyone. I'm sure if he were here, he would deliver this speech with greater passion and enthusiasm than I am able. But, in his absence, I will do my best to plant in you the seed of an idea that will capture the hearts and minds of every Chinese person as well as the people of all nations of the earth. It is an idea whose time has come, and whose place is here in China!

First, let me ask you. What is the value of a simple idea? Over the many centuries past, can we begin to measure the power or the expanse of ideas that have moved individuals and nations toward their destinies? It is said that an idea may be more powerful than the strongest army or economic and political force. Such powerful ideas create this strength and guide these forces.

The world is hungry for such ideas. The idea I am about to share with you will satisfy the largest of appetites; with the promise that China, Anhui Province, Hefei City, and the whole world will benefit by its acceptance and implementation. This idea embraces and supports all of China's economic development efforts including APEC, entering the WTO and winning the 2008 Olympic Games.

In preface to describing this idea, I would like to emphasize the dream of China becoming one of the world's greatest leading nations. The question is not if, but when. In order for China to become such, China must be a true leader—leading the way in creativity and innovation —a leader with integrity and a leader with vision.

*This idea's business development plan can initially be written and facilitated by the MBA students at USTC working together with students from all over the globe. This plan is now called "****U.N. Vision 2020.****" This name refers to both the year 2020 and to the term used for "perfect vision or perfect eyesight." It describes the development of a "new home" for the United Nations to be located near Hefei City. I've been told that one translation for the name Hefei means "where two rivers come together." What better place is there than here, for all nations to come together?*

Soon, the Olympic Games will be hosted in Beijing. Tourism will increase dramatically, and people from all over the world will come and discover and continue to develop the tremendous opportunities and advantages of doing business here. It is an opportune time for China to extend the invitation for the United Nations to come here and enjoy the long history, rich culture and abundant potential that China has to offer.

By the year 2020, the United Nations City will be the best planned and most modern city on the planet. Absent PowerPoint slides of impressive diagrams and beautiful pictures, let your imagination see a magnificent city surrounded by a Great Wall and landscaped with beautiful parks and golf courses, lakes and waterways. This city will include the following:

- *A most desirable international airport with flights from major cities around the world.*

- *The United Nations headquarters building to be established with the intent to become its home for the next 50 to 100 years.*

- *Consulate offices of various countries, including, housing, office and retail buildings, hotels and restaurants, theaters, churches and museums representing each country's unique architecture, decoration, and atmosphere.*

- *A U.N. University with the best international business and law schools, medical hospital and research center, language institutes and sports stadiums, along with all the necessary facilities to host future Olympic games and various kinds of international sports including western rodeos, American baseball, ice skating, and ice hockey, etc.*

- *As the world's largest tourist destination some of the supreme attractions will include one of the world's finest Disneyland theme parks, Water World, and zoos, etc., soon to be built and enjoyed.*

- *The U.N. Music & Arts Center, will be the next "Hollywood frontier" of music, art, film, entertainment and culture.*

- *Adventure and exercise centers for rock climbing, bungee jumping, swimming and weight lifting, along with various water sports and leisure activities on the connecting waterways and Lake Chao.*

- *Visitors will be able to tour the world in one city. The city's infrastructure will include:*

- *Futuristic elevated rail transportation systems with speed trains and super-highways coming from many major cities. Traffic will be facilitated and controlled as no other city has heretofore been able to do.*

- *There will be canals, elevators, people movers, walk ways, roadways with bike and running trails connecting everything from buildings, airport and sports centers etc.*

- *This one-of-a-kind city will have traditional, modern, and futuristic architecture and engineering designs of covered and connecting buildings using the best of construction materials with advanced heating, air conditioning and sound systems.*

This city will be the most unique and enviable city in the world. Truly, it will be "the best of the best" and the "most desirable city" in which to live. It will attract an unlimited abundance of economic and technological development. This unique city will join with Beijing, Shanghai, Shenzen and Hong Kong as another pillar of power and stability for China and the world.

May this idea be planted in your fertile soil and may it take root as you nourish it. And eventually, may it blossom and bear the fruit of unity, peace, and prosperity. Thank you very much for your attention.

Later one of my MBA students sent me the following e-mail:

Dear Dale Christensen.

Tuesday afternoon I opened my e-mail box and found your wife's "UN 2020 Vision" speech that I requested. I eagerly printed it and began to read. Wow! It is very exciting and full of great imaginations. When I finished and went back home, my father said, "Did you know the forum in Yellow Mountain? A teacher from your university—her name may be Mary—made a speech and believed that Hefei can host a UN City. It is a very good idea! Now everyone is talking about this. Do you know her?" I replied, "Yes! I knew her! Mary-Jo is my professor's wife! Just this afternoon my professor sent his plan to me. It is his idea!" My father smiled, "Your teacher is an imaginative man and very excellent!" Professor, you did a great thing! We were so proud of you! This week we are busy in preparing team discussion about Apple Computer Inc., and I have to say that this case is a long, big and complex story with many roles and events. We feel some difficulty, but we work very hard and believe we will finish it successfully! Thanks for your UN 2020 Vision again!

Sincerely, He Liang

The Anhui Evening Post, October 26, 2001, had the following headline and article translated here in English:

Build Hefei into a UN Capital

By the year 2020, make Hefei the new UN capital. This is a suggestion made by an American professor, Dale Christensen, and presented by his wife Mary-Jo, who is teaching in USTC this year. The idea, presented under the title "Project 2020," was one of the speeches invited by the Hefei city government for a forum held in Huangshan. She told the gathering that it is a part of the plan drafted by USTC MBA students. The plan was well built on persuasive arguments and details. Hefei is located at the joint of two rivers. This could symbolize the merge of human civilizations. The Hefei area is pleasant for living. In order to prepare it for the UN City, modern infrastructures should be developed. Hefei may apply directly to UN (for this designation). Though the suggestion sounds like a story from the Arabian Nights, why do not we make a dream? We all know 'no dream, no reality'. The talk touched off a lot of discussions among the participants.

I was thrilled to have the opportunity to offer a sense of pride and vision to the people of Hefei and of China. I'm certainly aware that many Americans are concerned about Chinese politics, Chinese business practices, and Chinese human rights. Like many emerging nations, China has had certain challenges and growing pains, but there is no denying that with the loosening of restrictions regarding capitalism and personal ambition, China will become one of the most dominant forces in the world over the next decades. This is already America's role, and I hope will we continue to be one of leadership, example, friendship and integrity.

ROYAL STAR

One of my MBA students, Robert Ye, the Vice President of Marketing for Rong Shi Da, a large manufacturing company (Maytag of China) approached me with a request to help come up with a new western name for the company. The only guideline was that it needed to sound like the Chinese name. After several days of work, I drafted every possibility. I narrowed the list to twenty and then the top ten. A week later, I gave this with my top three recommendations. The company chose my first choice "Royal Star". It was exciting to arrive at the airport some time later and see the large advertising billboards that name on it.

John & Dorothy Nanna

Mary-Jo Nanna (1 year)

Mary-Jo (3 years)

Riding Competition

High School Graduation

Engagement at Last

Christmas at the Nanna's

Wedding Day

Contemplating Our Future

At the White House - 1976

Family Picture - 1984

Cerro de Pasco, Peru - 1984

Mission Home in Lima, Peru - 1986

1993

Danbury, CT - 1993

1988 Farm Purchase

Campaigning for Pat Buchannan

Visiting the Great Wall of China

Signing a Contract with Chinese Partners

Posing with an MBA Class in Beijing

My Royalstar Logo at the Airport

Mexico - 1982

China - 2000

USTC - 2000

Anniversary - 2001

Yangshuo - 2002

Chapter 8

Final Years of Preparation

BACK IN AMERICA - AGAIN

Continuing my professorship, and with Mary-Jo teaching English classes, we lived in China until December of 2002. It was there that we suddenly found ourselves empty nesters, with each of our children in college or serving missions for the LDS Church. During our last months in the Far East I was able to establish important relationships between universities in China and universities in America, producing long-lasting benefits for both countries.

Our time in China taught us once again that the world is big and diverse. However, wherever you go, people have basically the same needs and ambitions. They love their families, and they want peace and prosperity. I'm proud that Americans have played a vital role in helping other nations and peoples of the world to be free and to live better lives. Moreover, I'm proud that the American republic has set an example of freedom, independence, and entrepreneurship that has inspired and motivated citizens of other countries to pursue similar dreams and visions for the future. Obviously, upon moving back to the United States, my ambition to continue to serve humanity in some capacity would continue.

EMPLOYMENT IN REAL-ESTATE

In January of 2003, shortly after returning to the States, I accepted a position in the Real Estate Division with the Corporation of the Presiding Bishop for the LDS Church. This division was responsible for acquiring and disposing of properties for chapels and other programs. Some leave their property to the Church in their wills. These residential and commercial properties are disposed of so funds can be put to use in other needful areas. The Church sponsors the largest non-governmental welfare organization in the world, growing and processing its own food, including farming and ranching operations. My job was making sure these acquisitions and dispersals went as efficiently and successfully as possible.

When I began working for the church in real estate, there were 15 projects. My first project was a 72-acre orchard that had been purchased many years previously by the Church for $200 an acre and was presently worth almost $140,000 an acre. This deal alone took almost a year to complete. At the height of my position as an employee of the LDS Church I had more than 260 separate projects I was working concurrently. We had a team that worked together. We were awesome as we were negotiating, processing and closing in an efficient and effective way.

I continued to work for the Church for three years in this capacity. However, as all good things must come to an end, in April of 2006 I once again felt drawn to pursue other objectives. Mary-Jo and I moved to Gallatin, Missouri, as we were drawn to our farm. We built our home on what was a corn field. Then we landscaped, put in a large garden, fruit trees, lawn, a tire swing hanging from a tree limb, picnic tables under the mulberry trees, a fire pit, and even a hammock.

COUNTRY LIFE

For many years Mary-Jo and I had dreamed about having a bed and breakfast so we could serve others as they travel. After all, we'd traveled for a considerable part of our lives, and we always really appreciated having a comfortable and affordable place to stay that was more than just a space to sleep. The seeds of that dream had begun as far back as 1988 with our purchase of the McKinsey farm in Jameson, Missouri. In 2006 we separated off some acreage and began to build a bed and breakfast that would be called the Marydale Inn. Our motto was "Come Roost with Us!"

The inn was built in stages. I designed the plans, put in the foundation and framed up the structure, including the roof. From then on Mary-Jo acted as the general contractor and coordinated everything to completion and operation. At that time, I was working full time in property management, so my availability to help with construction was limited to nights, weekends and vacations. Our daughter, Teresa, and her husband, Vance, stayed with us for about six months and helped us tremendously with the interior woodwork. The completed inn is approximately 9,400 square feet.

We opened Marydale Inn in March of 2009, and in December of that same year we hosted the inn's first wedding. Our guests included people from all over the world. They came to just get away, visit historical sites, or visit the Amish community of nearby Jamesport. Our inn is still in business today. Our property includes a corral, pastures, ponds, pens, and a barn so our guests can enjoy the rural experiences of interacting with farm animals, fishing, star gazing, bird watching, swinging from the hanging swings on the wraparound porch and enjoying long walks in the woods. We want Marydale Inn to be a peaceful piece of heaven on earth. My sister, Dian, and her husband, Art, have taken over as innkeepers so Mary-Jo and I could live yet another adventure.

A MISSION TO NEW YORK

We loved our mission serving in Peru and had prepared for many years to serve another mission as a senior couple. We were prepared to go wherever we were assigned in the world. In August, we traveled to New York and Connecticut to attend a family wedding. While walking the streets of Manhattan, Mary-Jo and I both had strong feelings about serving in New York City. During October of 2012, we felt strong impressions that we ought to serve now and immediately began the application process. In the comments section of our application we indicated that we had a strong desire to serve in Italy where Mary-Jo's ancestors are from. Unknown to me, Mary-Jo had also written New York City because of the experience we had there. Our real desire was to serve wherever the Lord wanted us.

In the midst of all this, we invested in a new business. We organized a limited liability company and drafted our operations agreement with experienced herb growers with future plans to raise tilapia fish and incorporate hydroponics etc. We had been discussing this for a long time and anticipate a bright future.

When the call came, it was to the New York New York North Mission, Once again, we felt at peace and at home. In early April of 2013 Mary-Jo and I arrived at our new missionary headquarters in the New York New York North Mission. Our residence for the next year was in East Harlem.

It's from this vantage point that I started to prepare this manuscript, based on material I've been gathering for decades. As our eighteen-month mission to the people of the Big Apple draws to a close, the time feels right to finally launch my campaign as the dark horse candidate for President of the United States.

RUN FOR WHAT?

Knowing what our Founding Fathers did for us, I am forced to consider what I am leaving behind for future generations. I'm grateful for the heritage my parents and past generations gave me. As I contemplate this, I want to do everything in my power to do the same for my posterity. Past generations left Americans an opportunity and a dream. We must now individually go to our own mountain, so to speak, to receive guidance in determining for ourselves what we will give to those who follow after us.

Many times, I have gone to my mountain. Again and again, I've returned with the same feeling of urgency (purpose, mission, focus, or mantle). After great deliberation, while still in New York on our mission, I finally told my wife about my struggle and my conclusion. Her response was to verbalize the reality of what I was struggling with.

"You think you should run for President of the United States?" Mary-Jo queried, and then continued, "You're not a Senator or a governor. You're not rich enough or well-known enough to be seriously considered. Why would others vote for you when you are not a well-connected professional politician or had years of large organization leadership experience?"

My ego took the first of many blows on that first day. It was difficult, even though I knew what she said represented my current reality. I responded, "I don't know. I just know that I must do this."

"Well, if you run a negative campaign, even I won't vote for you," she countered.

We just looked at each other for a long time. She was sitting at the kitchen table, and I was turned sideways in my chair in front of the computer. I was halfway through the list of things I'd need to do to get started when I was overcome by a feeling of hopelessness. It all seemed to be just too much—impossible.

I took a deep breath and said, "Mary-Jo, I don't intend to run a typical campaign like all the others. My campaign will be quite different. I want to focus on the big issues, the key issues that need to be addressed before all the other things can be solved. Some of these issues are non-negotiable. I'll be inviting people to turn to the Constitution as their 'standard of liberty' by which to measure me and all other candidates, programs, and solutions."

"But," asked Mary-Jo, "you haven't held even one important political office. How do you expect anyone to take you seriously?"

I was not surprised, but a little disappointed to hear her talk like this because we had discussed this very topic even before we were married.

"Just like everything I have done before. I know that you believe that 'with God, all things are possible.' If I am with him and doing his will, this will be possible. If I speak the truth, others will recognize it and do their part. This is not a one-man show. It will take over 75 million people to make this happen. But, with faith, hard work, and with God, it can happen. It must happen."

We continued discussing this for several hours that morning and again on many following days. At some point, I found myself trying to explain that it was actually an advantage for me not to be rich, famous or powerful. The United States has had enough of that, and it's not working. In reality these great strengths have become our biggest weaknesses.

At the end of another long day and exhausted, we laid down to sleep. At this time, we were still on our LDS mission in New York. The next day, after an inspiring meeting with other missionaries, we met some very interesting people on the streets of Harlem and continued with our missionary work. Teaching our evening English class was the highlight of the day. Many students were making great progress. That evening, before we turned off the lights, my conversation with Mary-Jo migrated from a discussion of past accomplishments to one of future campaigning possibilities. Mary-Jo was seeking assurance that it was actually possible for us to enter, let alone win, such a campaign to be President of the United States.

"Mary-Jo, don't you remember what I used to tell my MBA students in China?" I asked.

"No. What?" she asked as she tried to remember.

"Well, when the students seemed to doubt their abilities, I tried to give them confidence by helping them see their potential. 'Think of China,' I would say. Then I would ask them, 'What is China's biggest problem?' Their answer was always the same. With concern, they would say, 'Too many people!' We'd discuss that for a few minutes and then I would ask them another question: 'What is China's greatest asset?' They also always enthusiastically replied, 'China has a huge market!' So, you see, their biggest weakness is also their biggest strength. I feel it is the same with me. My biggest problem is not being rich, famous or powerful, but I believe that this is also my greatest strength."

"Wow!" she replied, and then exhaled, "I know that's true?"

"Absolutely!" I said with absolute confidence. I'm ready for a change. All we have to do is convince 75 million Americans to vote for me, and we can make the changes that are needed,"

We talked for another hour.

"OK, Mary-Jo, so what's it going to be? Are you going to vote for me or not?" Her response was, "From the time we first spoke of this before we were married, I knew you could and would be a fantastic president. You are gifted in your political understanding. This leaves me in awe. Your practical, common sense experience, having lived in different states and countries, having a variety of professional experiences, etc., etc. make you a very desirable and capable candidate. You wholeheartedly have my vote and my support."

It's about time we had a President who followed the Constitution rather than just drag it along. For the past fifty years, each President has stretched the limits of presidential authority. Sadly, the other branches of government have been willing accomplices whenever their party is in the White House. Even sadder, many Americans expect, and even demand, such abuse of power. I believe it is possible to elect a president who will do what the Constitution requires and be disciplined enough *not* to do what it does not allow.

CRITICAL OBSERVATIONS

Going back to 2008, like most other Americans, I watched the financial crisis unfold with the real estate market crash, the halt of construction for lack of capital, and the dramatic economic slowdown. Simultaneously, there was a Wall Street meltdown and financial fear around the world, resulting in more instability. The stagnation in business affected everyone, including my family and friends and their families and friends.

A part of me couldn't help but think that we were getting exactly what we deserved because of our pride, greed and selfishness. Society seems to be more divided and drawing closer to what some are calling "Civil War II – A Popular and Predictable Polarization." This is another whole topic for a future discussion.

In the brewing conflict, the issue is not over the slavery of others, but over enslaving oneself by substances like liquor, drugs (legal and illegal), gambling and the corrosive media practices like pornography. This captivity may even include certain philosophies or ideas that are so passionately held by some that those who hold contrary views are bullied and threatened with retaliation in many forms, including violence. Materialistic pride, gluttony and drunkenness are enslaving the national spirit of independence, self-reliance and self-determination. Some among the succeeding generation have little or no appreciation for the sacrifices of prior generations. We have squandered and polluted many of our natural resources as well as our personal physical and moral purity.

There are also a myriad of social and economic addictions in the world. The divisions between people are escalating in many ways. Politically, it is democracy versus a republic, right versus left, conservatives versus liberals, etc. Economically, it is the haves versus the have-nots. Morally, the divisions are between religious and non-religious, pornography versus free speech, pro-abortion versus pro-life, and honesty versus copyright infringement.

There is continuing and perhaps accelerating division along ethnic and racial lines. The words of Abraham Lincoln ring as true today as when he first uttered them:

> "*A house divided against itself cannot stand. I believe this government cannot endure permanently half-slave and half-free. I do not expect the Union to be dissolved—I do not expect the house to fall—but I do expect it will cease to be divided. It will become all one thing or all the other.*"

Over the last few decades the public seems to have lost more and more confidence in politicians who practice what I term political prostitution, a desire to gain power or money for themselves and others rather than a genuine desire to serve this nation. Politicians continue to vote themselves higher salaries while increasing taxes and the size of government during a struggling economy. Their purposes attempt to guarantee success and prosperity for everyone. Their programs provide free benefits and services to many who are not willing to work. Those who need help should receive it at a local or state level. I consider this trend as part of an insidious plan, which is part of a greater lie that will accelerate the destruction of America and its freedoms.

In spite of these pessimistic outlooks, I remember one brilliant observation in a certain political ad by a local woman running for public office. She stated in her ad that she was not going to call illegal aliens undocumented workers. She would also not call thieves undocumented owners, drug dealers undocumented pharmacists, or drop outs undocumented graduates. I enjoyed and supported that ad, but does this ad mean that her victory would translate into a true commitment to follow through on such principles?

Like many Americans, I find myself skeptical of any politician who makes big promises. I'm one who does not believe our current struggle can be defined as Republican vs. Democrat or liberal vs. conservative. It seems to me that the entire political system needs an overhaul. No matter the political viewpoint or affiliation, one party seems no different from the other when it comes to continuing the same self-serving policies that have infected the country for almost a century. Anyone elected to political office is immediately beholden to the political constituencies that got them there. If anyone is going to finally cut out this cancer, the citizens of America need to be prepared for serious surgery and some long-term rehabilitation. And it will likely involve factors that few politicians have the courage to acknowledge: pain and sacrifice.

The bailing out of certain favored financial institutions by the American government so they (the institutions and government) can continue to own more of the American Dream has been particularly disturbing to me. Thomas Jefferson was prophetic when he said, "I believe that banking institutions are more dangerous to our liberties than standing armies . . . If the American people ever allow private banks to control the issue of their currency, first by inflation, then by deflation, the banks and corporations that will grow up . . . will deprive the people of all property until their children wake up homeless on the continent their fathers conquered."

It has been agonizing to witness over the course of my life a weakening of the U.S. Constitution and the undermining of American sovereignty by the United Nations. I've watched a continuing expansion of foreign commitments and taxpayer investment in huge non-loyal, multi-national companies. Increasing illegal immigration divides our citizens. Larger amounts of capital continue to flow out of the country. Education has become a massive industry, with universities fostering the notion of an elite aristocracy among its parent and student customers. Many public schools for children and youth are failing their customers (the students). More and more students are graduating with huge student loans and finding it more and more difficult to find jobs with salaries sufficient to pay them off. They are being invited into debt without the ability to get out.

The United States has more citizens serving sentences in prison than any other nation on earth. As a result, these places often become overcrowded universities of crime. Moreover, this industry's dangerous curriculum is being taught with free tuition paid for by the U.S. taxpayers.

The massive media propaganda machines make it continually less popular to foster religious conviction, advertising the idea that religious belief is founded in bigotry and ignorance. As a result, those who have religious conviction are marked and treated more and more like a persecuted sect. Traditional celebrations such as Christmas and Easter have been under savage attack by a very vocal minority who proclaim that such practices offend their own desire to live in a religion-free world. There are those fighting against the freedom founded on the Judeo-Christian traditions, in spite of the fact that they are the very foundation and pillars of our Constitution and laws.

Nevertheless, rather than only complain about the situation, we must move forward, while being long-suffering and tolerant. All Americans must be permitted to believe as they choose to believe, even as certain constituencies strive to deprive others of the same privilege.

My personal role and goal is to serve others and protect our freedom. In a free nation, we can encourage each other to perform good deeds, cheer up the sad, make miracles happen in the lives of others, and share our bounty and blessings. We can support each other in efforts to heal and comfort the sick and downtrodden, make new friends, and pray for our enemies.

My continuing thoughts and admonitions to all regarding these days of looming debt and possible slavery in which we now live are:

1. Be united and patriotic;
2. Stay out of debt;
3. Have an emergency plan that will provide our families with basic needs.

There is always the possibility of temporary or long term disruption of general services like food, water, power or transportation and catastrophic climate/health issues or explosive social unrest.

A POPULAR AND PREDICTABLE POLARIZATION

Almost 150 years ago, our nation entered into a devastating conflict that divided the nation and many families. The campaign to maintain states' rights and to limit slavery was at the heart of this rebellion. Today, the question of slavery is again being asked. Does any individual or any organization have the right to own another individual? The answer of course is NO! Yet many individuals are agreeing to become slaves. Sadly, we observe slavery then and slavery now. Everywhere we look, we see soaring individual debt and a mounting national debt. We are allowing ourselves to be brought into bondage every bit as much as the children of Israel when they chose to stay in Egypt after the seven-year famine was over.

As stated earlier, there are many already bound in servitude to social, economic, and physical addiction. A growing number are weighted down by the chains of pornography, promiscuity, and human trafficking. Among the average American populace, there is a growing ignorance of the Constitution, and apathy towards our patriotic roots. Principled statesmanship is being replaced by political prostitution, moral poverty, and economic obesity. Liberty and justice for all are being traded for universal security and global citizenship. In some parts of the world, this trend includes ethnic cleansing and violence against their own. Natural resources are being exploited and abused and the environment polluted, while our individual rights are squandered and national sovereignty is jeopardized.

The conflict is not just geographical. Nor are the battles all fought by battalions or with bombs, ships and planes. This is a moral and spiritual war being waged by individuals who are fighting for command and ownership of their own souls. The battle is for truth and liberty, and if we are defeated it means slavery. Some now unashamedly call evil good and good evil. Champions of deceit hide behind the law to promote exploitation and rob others of their inalienable rights.

Here we are, 150 years after the first Civil War, having enjoyed periods of prosperity and peace. Once again we find ourselves in a conflict that divides our nation and its families. Slavery is also at the heart of this rebellion and its resolution is the answer to the same question: "Who can own you? Who can own your body, your mind or your soul? Your answer, commitment and action will determine the outcome of this next great Civil War II.

MY PATRIOTIC VALUES

The following are my long-time declared *Patriotic Values*:

1. **God created this world.** He has given us inalienable rights. He has assisted in righteous causes and blessed righteous people throughout history, but He does not ignore the free agency of mankind.
2. **America is a promised and blessed land.** This land was preserved and prepared as a cradle of freedom. It has been preserved at times by Divine Providence. It was difficult to achieve freedom, and it will be a struggle to preserve it. If Americans are righteous they will prosper, be blessed, and remain free. History is the result of the choices made by others. The future will be a result of our choices. It is necessary and good to protect life, liberty and property. The United States of America is sovereign and stands separate from all other nations.
3. **The Declaration of Independence and the U.S. Constitution were inspired of God.** God raised up and supported the Founding Fathers who expressed their grievances, declared independence, fought for

liberty, and drafted and accepted the standard of liberty for the world. There is wisdom in not straying from the original intent and text of the U.S. Constitution. It was intended to limit the role and power of government. There have been changes that have weakened the Constitution. Every citizen must defend, protect and preserve this sacred document.

4. **Law is essential for the governance of humankind.** Governments are instituted of God for the benefit of man. However, when unchecked, most individuals and all governments will abuse power. One day God will hold those in power accountable for their acts in relationship to making and administering laws for the good and safety of society. Governments have the right to enact laws to secure the public interest while protecting each individual's free exercise of conscience and religious belief, the right to control property, and to protect life. Governments should not interfere in foreign countries. Crimes should be punished according to the nature of the offense.

5. **Governments and citizens have sacred duties.** Public officials must enforce the law and administer justice as they uphold the voice of the people. Citizens are bound to obey the laws of the land and sustain and uphold the government that protects them. It is not right to mingle religious influence with civil government in order to favor one religious—or non-religious—society over another. However, it is right, good, and even essential to have reverence and righteous influence and discussion in government. Citizens should appeal to civil law for the redress of wrongs; nonetheless, we are justified in self-defense. Citizens should seek out and support honest, wise, and good people to serve in public office. Public service is a sacred honor and

responsibility requiring sacrifice. Our country and citizens should be examples of strength, freedom and personal liberty and should inspire others to be like us, but never try to force them to be like us.

6. **There are evil powers trying to destroy liberty.** Throughout the history of the world, there have been those who have tried to suffocate liberty. This struggle between good and evil, and between freedom and tyranny, continues today. Citizens must be vigilant in watching for these dangers that are among us or will come among us and fight against secret and evil forces attempting to get power and gain. Citizens must avoid moral relativism and warn others. If America becomes corrupt or supports these evils—such as organized crime in all its diverse distinctions, including cybercrime— we will slowly, but surely, sacrifice our hard-fought freedoms and allow ourselves to be devastated.

In upcoming chapters I will set forth my political platform for all Americans to analyze and dissect according to their own preferences and perspectives. I hope many of my ideas will be seen as refreshing, exciting and a sincere attempt to adopt many of the best ideas from both sides of the political aisle. My vision is admittedly quite ambitious, but it is my goal to convince the citizens of this nation that such a balanced approach to political reform is not only achievable, but imperative to the survival of the United States of America.

Viewing the Grand Canyon - 2002

50th Birthday Party - 2003

Marydale Inn - 2009

2010 · Enjoying Lake Candlewood

Fishing on the Farm

Riding Eva and Sweet Pea

NY, NY North Mission

Missionary Companions
- 2013

Family Reunion - 2013

Our High Priest Group in Harlem 2nd Ward

Chapter 9

Path of a Patriot

THE VISION

There were times when my parents and other patient teachers needed to discipline me. This discipline included an occasional scolding or spanking. When my heart was broken and my eyes filled with tears, they would put their arms around me and remind me that I could be a "good boy." They told me that I had so much potential and just needed to channel it in the right direction.

I can vividly see their beautiful faces with loving eyes and kind words saying, "Dale, you are a born leader. You can and must be the kind of person that others will want to follow." I sincerely believed them, and a vision opened up in my mind of who I was and the kind of person I could become. I have remembered their words and tried to follow their advice, even when I made mistakes. I have tried to follow these objectives in life, school, sports, work and worship.

So many times, the memories of these people have continued to influence me and help me correct my mistakes and chart my course in life. They still inspire me to rise to my loftiest heights, challenging me along the way to be true to myself and help others to do the same.

REVIEWING MY CHOICES

I don't believe that our choices in life are predestined. Much of it depends upon our choices and our efforts. I strive to follow the Savior and make sound choices that will engender the best results. It's been my lifelong experience that choices made with pure and righteous intentions clear the mind, open doors, shield a person from evil, and light a pathway to the future. It's critical that we do not take our power of choice for granted because it is up to us to discover our greatness and determine our destiny.

My life, as with every other human life, has been filled with many choices—countless decisions and crossroads. I have not always made the best choices. Along the way, some bad choices have cost me happiness, prosperity, and other blessings. I feel fortunate that I have very few examples of regret; nevertheless I'll recount a few. I regret that I did not complete my Eagle in Boy Scouts when I went to England. I regret that I did not complete my last year of law school when I left to campaign in Kansas and began working as an investment acquisitions specialist. I regret not having gone on to obtain a PhD in Political Science. At that time, we were called to serve Peru. At the time, there were extenuating circumstances that seemed like good excuses, but I no longer accept them. I just didn't make the choices I should have, and I must live with the consequences. I believe our experiences here on earth are a test of growth and development that prepares us for much greater things in this life and in the life to come. So, I keep moving forward with the hope that I will eventually realize certain visions.

On the brighter side, I'm grateful that I *did* follow through with certain vital decisions and choices. These actions have made all the difference. Sometimes choices were easy because one of my brothers or sisters led the way. I also had special friends and other heroes who served as powerful examples. They were (and are) wise men and women who have invited me, repeatedly, to surpass even my own expectations.

I'm proud of those moments in my life when I willfully elected to leave my comfort zone and explore the world. One of the first such decisions was during my senior year of high school when I left my home and family to live in London, England, and later to work in Rotterdam, the Netherlands. These were life-changing experiences that shaped my thinking and helped me to realize that I had abilities of great worth. I'm grateful that I chose to serve a two-year mission in New England for The Church of Jesus Christ of Latter-day Saints.

I chose to play freshman football at Brigham Young University in Provo, Utah, and basketball at Dixie College in St. George, Utah, then transferred to and graduated from Boston College in Massachusetts, where I met my wife Mary-Jo. I went on to pursue an MBA there, and then, with Mary-Jo's support, to study law and work on Capital Hill in Washington, D.C. Several times over the years, even with various opportunities to pursue public office hovering virtually over my head, I chose not to run.

Without a doubt, one of the decisions for which I am most grateful was the choice of my companion, Mary-Jo Nanna, and our decision together to be married and sealed for time and all eternity in the temple. In time, this decision led to the blessing of four wonderful children. On May 14, 2014, Mary-Jo and I celebrated our fortieth wedding anniversary.

I chose to work in several professions, including commercial real estate, sales and training, education, business and property management. Each has offered to me valuable perspectives on life and service, but none more powerful than choosing to accept a call to serve, along with my wife, a three-year mission for my church in Lima, Peru, and an eighteen-month mission in Harlem, New York, and Danbury, Connecticut. Our intention is to yet serve additional missions in other parts of the world for the rest of our lives.

IMPRESSIONS

It was during the ninth month of our mission in Harlem (in December 2013) that strong impressions of public service flooded back into my heart. Vivid ideas of political involvement began to burn brightly and urgently in my mind.

Sketchy notes and comments unrelated to our duties as missionaries began to appear in my journal entries. Finally, I determined that I should discuss these impressions with Mary-Jo. She listened with great understanding and cautious expectation. So many times over the years we had discussed this topic, but the notion had always been put off for another day. We began a process of prayer and fasting together to gain greater wisdom with regard to this issue. Nevertheless, the moments of enlightenment—ideas and impressions of how to conduct a campaign and serve in the office to which I will be elected—continued in frequency and with increased intensity.

One day in the barbershop in East Harlem, a mutual friend chatted about her feelings regarding the 2012 presidential election and the current state of the Union. She did not realize it, but at that moment she kindled a fire in my heart that forced me to the farthest edge of decision-making. She and her husband were very professional and polite, but I left their establishment somewhat troubled and bubbling in turmoil.

THE CRUCIBLE

Mary-Jo and I agonized, discussed, and debated over all the ramifications of running for the President of the United States of America. She was concerned about the costs of such a campaign. She wished now that I had been getting political experience over the years, like all the other candidates. She asked me to ponder, sincerely and fairly, how I was even conventionally qualified to be accepted as a candidate for office, let alone be president? It may have been the most important question that I could have ever been asked, because the answer, when it came, "Rocked my world." In any case, the answer filled me with incredible joy and satisfaction.

There were many sleepless nights after late-night conversations regarding different aspects of the topic. How would such a campaign, and even the job itself, affect our marriage, our children, and family? What would our friends and extended family think of such a decision? Many already might think that we were a bit eccentric for having led the life that we had lived.

Would our decision to run for office mean that we would be slandered and ridiculed? Would such a decision place me or my family in serious physical danger? Could I be killed? Could our children be kidnapped? Would my church be embarrassed by us? Would my political philosophy even fit into the mold of what seems to be accepted by today's political environment? What kind of a campaign would we be able to organize and successfully manage to the very end? What would it cost? And, would we even want to fund a campaign similar to the kind that everyone else ran?

Mary-Jo and I were both happy to be serving together as missionaries, but this political interference became very stressful and consuming. I was going through the daily motions of missionary work and loving it, but there seemed to be a continuous background noise running in my head. Every night I went to sleep, and every morning I woke up thinking about all the speeches, interviews, debates, strategies, challenges, and then the necessary presidential actions that I would need to undertake in the office itself.

At times, I likened these thoughts and feelings to those of a CEO of a budding technological startup company and all the steps he would need to overcome to bring his product to market. Or, I likened the stress to that of a military general considering the logistics of a great upcoming battle. It began to feel almost like a game of chess, trying to always play with the confidence that you are fully aware of your next ten moves. I'm reminded of the saying, "There are three kinds of people: the few that make things happen; the many who watch things happen; and then there are those who just wonder what happened." I must try to make things happen. To do otherwise is not an alternative.

During the Christmas and New Year's holiday season, I fell very ill with a serious cold and cough. I got better for a few days and then relapsed. Not wanting to contaminate other missionaries or the people that we visited, I decided to stay home and recover. It was during these days that I used much of my time for thinking and writing. Mary-Jo continued to go out and do what she could to take care of us and keep the missionary spirit alive and well.

THE DECISION

One day, I was thinking about so many great people who had changed the world for the better. These individuals often focused on a simple and true message and specific mission.

One person *can* make a difference and succeed in what seems to be impossible. Whether or not he or she ever realized it or even admitted it, I believe the success was always aided by Divine intervention.

At some point, and I can't say when this moment actually arrived, I concluded that I must move forward with faith and let the consequences follow. Mary-Jo and I had made it a matter of considerable prayer and finally decided it was just the right thing to do. I continued receiving feelings of urgency, excitement, and peace about our decision. We both felt that it was the right thing for *us* to do and that God would raise up people as necessary who would help us in this great undertaking.

The first such person to join me was Lee Gibbons, a website expert with an impressive resume of success in his industry. He designed and constructed a website to help us understand how we could run a unique campaign and win the election. The second person was Chris Heimerdinger, an author of more than twenty books, who aided me in the structure of this autobiography.

THE INTERVIEW

Some weeks after the convictions began to sink in; we began to feel almost overwhelmed. We had an interview with our mission president. Timidly, we shared with him what we had been experiencing and doing. He patiently listened as we described all of our impressions and concerns.

He wore what we perceived to be a visible mantle of authority and had piercing wisdom shining in his eyes. We told him that we would do whatever he recommended. If he felt that we should wait until October, when our mission came to its conclusion, before we did anything to prepare for the campaign, we would forget about it for a few more months and wait. On the contrary, President Morgan enthusiastically encouraged us to proceed. Then he said, "Not only should you move forward with faith, but you should ask the Lord, 'What more? Is there anything more that I should do or know?'"

Mary-Jo and I looked at each other and then back to him in gratitude. We felt relief and a gentle confirmation that we were not "out of bounds" or doing something wrong. Perhaps I was only one of many—that is to say, we were *two* of many (I've never considered any undertaking unilaterally, without Mary-Jo's full support at my side)—who were being similarly guided or prepared. If so, then so be it. We will move forward and do our part, however great or small.

A NEW PLEDGE OF ALLEGIANCE

Up to this point, this book has focused upon my life story and how I came to this place in my life where I was finally willing to throw my hat in the ring and run for our nation's highest office. It's time now to "open up," so to speak, or perhaps just summarize, some of the general information that defines who I am as a person. It's that definition, I believe, that will be paramount in eliciting the confidence necessary from the citizens of the United States of America regarding my qualifications for President.

The most important attribute that I believe I bring to this office—and unfortunately one of the most forgotten, downplayed, and undermined attributes that should define the public's perception of American politics—is *trust*. Voters need to know that I have no constituencies, no burdensome financial debts, no hobbling political debts, and the freedom of being absolutely un-beholden to any person, lobby, or organization. Well, let me back that up slightly. I *do* feel indebted and beholden to one thing, and that is the U.S. Constitution.

I am, I enthusiastically confess, a Constitutionalist. Yet I feel I have to be careful placing even that kind of a label upon myself because the term has come to mean different things to different people. In an effort to simplify my core meaning, I'll just say that I believe the United States Constitution is a monumental, sublime—and yes—even inspired document. It was fought for, toiled over, and carefully formulated utilizing principles handed down from the most enlightened thinkers dating back to the ancient Greeks, and even the Old Testament and the first five books of Moses or the Torah. Our Founding Fathers were intimately familiar with and well-versed in the most revered philosophers of the Reformation and Enlightenment that were directly connected with the world's emergence from the Dark Ages. These philosophers included John Locke of England, Charles Montesquieu and Jean-Jacques Rousseau of France, as well as many others. Our Founding Fathers deeply invested in designing and blue printing the best form of earthly government. Some fully recognized that only God himself could ever bestow an absolutely perfect form of government for mankind. Nevertheless, they strived for and *prayed* for a system of governance that could grant us the ability to be free and achieve our loftiest potential as human beings, despite the fact that we are perpetually surrounded and besieged by imperfect and sometimes evil men who seek our downfall. Our Founding Fathers sought to implement the same goals as the Renaissance philosophers. The difference for Washington, Jefferson, Madison, Franklin, Adams, and the philosophers was that their philosophies would not be bound inside the pages of books and treatises to be used for reference only. These men actually intended to lay out the political blueprint of a free republic and then implement those principals in practice.

Here are some statements from some our most revered statesmen regarding the Constitution of the United States:

"I consider the foundation of the Constitution as laid on this ground: that 'all powers not delegated to the United States by the Constitution . . . are reserved to the states or to the people . . . To take a single step beyond the boundaries thus specifically drawn around the powers of Congress is to take possession of a boundless field of power, no longer susceptible of any definition."

- Thomas Jefferson

"Don't interfere with anything in the constitution. That must be maintained, for it is the only safeguard of our liberties."

- Abraham Lincoln

"The Constitution only guarantees the American people the right to pursue happiness. You have to catch it yourself."

- Benjamin Franklin

There are so many similar quotes from James Madison, Thomas Paine, George Washington, and countless others. All of them emphasized the paramount importance of this document. The Constitution of the United States has inspired freedom and prosperity for more than two hundred years. Other nations have used it as the model upon which they established their own constitutions. It's my conviction that it was established under the guidance of an omnipotent hand, and it was intended that it should be maintained for the rights and protection of all people on the earth.

Today, I fear too many Americans have forgotten the toils, sacrifices, compromises, and inspiration that lie at the root of this document. The Founding Fathers were even wise enough to recognize that time and changes in society might necessitate future amendments, or in other words, the Constitution should be open to superior ideas that would better incorporate the basic principles outlined in the main body of the Constitution. Many of these amendments have been no less inspired than the Constitution itself.

However, it is my position that *some* amendments were *not* inspired, and in fact ignored the very principles that the Constitution sought to protect. Those amendments that weaken individual liberty or strengthen governmental power ought to be repealed. I'll elaborate upon this matter in upcoming chapters. The point is that the Constitution, at its core, is the basis for my political platform, and I recognize it as the supreme law of the land.

With this perspective in mind, I would like to propose a serious alteration to this nation's Pledge of Allegiance—the very statement that so many school children have recited since their earliest years in school. My pledge of allegiance is as follows: "I pledge allegiance to the Constitution of the United States of America and to the flag and to the republic for which it stands, one nation under God, indivisible, with liberty and justice for all."

The *Constitution*—not the flag—should be the most important part of our pledge of allegiance. Without the Constitution, the flag could represent anything to anyone, and the republic could be transformed into something completely different from what the Founding Fathers established or envisioned. The United States Constitution is the supreme law of the land. It is the republic's anchor, rudder, and steering wheel. It is our only hope.

WHO WE ARE, AND WHO I AM

As citizens of this country, we are all part of one massive family. Every one of us has personal challenges and concerns. No matter what your needs or concerns might be, no matter what your age, race, sex, marital status or lifestyle, you have been gifted certain inalienable rights from God, including, as Thomas Jefferson put so eloquently, life, liberty, and the pursuit of happiness. Regardless of your party, political philosophy, or political preferences, the U.S. Constitution protects these rights through proper government organization and function.

As I unfold my political platform, some may be offended by the candid bluntness of my positions, others might be offended by the surprisingly liberal nature of some of my ideas. In any case, I believe my positions are Constitutional. I will do my best to buttress my views and opinions in each individual instance.

I've made it no secret from the outset of this book to reveal that I am a Mormon, or more accurately, a member of The Church of Jesus Christ of Latter-day Saints. In my experience as a missionary and in other venues of life I've certainly encountered the passionate and stubborn intolerance of some towards my religion. I consider it unfortunate that in most instances this prejudice has been expressed by fellow Christians. In an effort to address that concern, I can only testify that I know God lives and that His son, Jesus Christ, is the Savior of the world and the light of my life. In the LDS faith we don't use the phrase "born again" in the same way or as frequently as some Protestant faiths, but I feel and believe in the vital principle this phrase communicates. I accept its precepts and adhere to the doctrine. I know that I personally have been "born again" in the best tradition of how I believe Jesus Christ meant that phrase in John, Chapter 3. I am Christ's disciple and I love Him and want to follow Him in earnest._

I also want to make it clear again that I've never held public office. Unlike so many other presidents and candidates, I am not a practicing attorney. In today's political climate I consider both of these facts to be *virtues* and *advantages*. It's unfortunate that we've created a system that seems to necessitate such criteria in every citizen who seeks to run for public office, which includes being President. Some fully believe that to be effective, one must intimately understand the political climate of Washington, D.C., the wheelers and dealers, who's in and who's out, and other protocols and traditions of the three great branches of our republic. This is nonsense. I intend to show through my platform that it's exactly this perspective that continues to perpetuate circumstances in our country that could lead to its downfall. Despite not being a practicing attorney, I have studied law, and I have spent a lifetime studying the Constitution. I certainly concede and propose that a president must be a powerful and dynamic leader. However, more importantly, I believe a president should be person of unwavering principle, conviction, and trust. Those are the qualifications I intend to bring to the office.

Readers should also know that I'm not a military veteran. When I was young I certainly made myself available for the draft and for military service in the Vietnam War. If I had been called up, I would have proudly served. My Uncle Henry had been in the Army, but I had always wanted to be a fighter pilot like my older brother.

I'm also not a famous movie or sports personality. Although I certainly believe that all Americans have a right to express their views and opinions, I've often been surprised at how those famous in areas outside of policy or politics can influence far more people than one would logically expect. Sadly, their greatest influence is on the youth, who are most susceptible to political manipulation.

Lastly, I've done my best throughout my life to provide for my wife and children. I've been richly blessed, but I certainly don't fit into the category of the powerful and wealthy. I've changed careers more than once, and many years of my life have also been devoted to service and charity. I grew up in a humble home and my personal value system placed little emphasis on the ambition of wealth. That part of my American Dream has always been alive and well, but I've also been willing to sacrifice financial gains at times to serve others. It's always been my view—a view reinforced by experience—that the Lord blesses those who give service to their fellow men. He provides them with precisely what they need, when they need it. This doesn't mean that those who serve can avoid the sweat of hard work. We must always rely on our skills and intelligence and strive for a good education or vocation. What I mean to say is that, ultimately, our lives are in Divine hands. I'll pray and have faith that everything depends on God, and then I'll do all I can as if everything depends on me.

What I want readers to know is that I love America, I understand leadership, and I understand business from its highest corporate levels to the most menial and humble mom-and-pop establishments. I have the heart of a teacher, and I see becoming President as a natural outgrowth of my sincere desire to serve tirelessly and selflessly. I feel I can honestly say that I don't care about financial or social enrichment. My objective, pure and simple, is to do everything in my power to save the Constitution and to strengthen individual citizens and the republic of the United States. I'll spend the rest of this book painting my vision of how I will turn this dream into a reality.

Chapter 10

Guide to Freedom

THE FORMULA

When Thomas Paine described the dark days of the American Revolutionary War, he wrote, "These are the times that try men's souls." I believe the circumstances then were no more dire than the circumstances we face today. For many decades Americans have devalued Constitutional freedoms with what some might define as more "modern" or "updated" philosophies of socialistic democracy and evolving socialism. Like many American entrepreneurs, businessmen and economists, I believe America's economy may, at this moment, be standing upon the most fragile footing in its long history.

For example, the national media confirms that our national debt is greater than at any other time in history. The current administration has increased our debt more than any other administration in history. The previous administration did almost the same thing. Yet very few Americans understand the implications of these monetary decisions and the ramifications of this debt. We go on with our lives, taking for granted our luxuries, our pastimes, and even our excessive frivolities with the full belief that nothing will ever really change, certainly not permanently.

I believe this state of mind—being lulled into this sense of false security—is a recipe for disaster. What no one wants to hear about are the tough decisions and actions that will bring about real and lasting solutions. Here is a fact: fixing this problem will require resolve, sacrifice and pain.

Some will undoubtedly conclude that expressing this so bluntly will condemn my campaign. So be it! I will not lie to the American people! Changes are coming. The question is: will America wake up soon enough and recognize the seriousness of our situation? Will Americans elect leaders who can guide us through this fiery crucible and keep our freedoms intact? Or will we continue to gradually surrender our freedoms to smooth-talking deceivers who sway us into believing that we don't have to sacrifice anything, thinking that the problems will resolve themselves, and life will go on exactly as it always has. The cost of this state of mind is much higher than we can imagine. The price is our peace, our liberty, and perhaps even our lives.

As it becomes obvious that certain freedoms are being forfeited, some will try to convince us that these inconveniences are only temporary. My fear is that too many are buying into such falsehoods. I'm here to plead with and convince all citizens that we do not have to, nor can we afford to, sacrifice our freedoms. My role as President will be to join with others to help guide our nation through these painful transitions as smoothly as possible. However, I believe it's unavoidable that we *will* have to sacrifice some of the creature comforts that too many have come to think are perpetually available and theirs by entitlement, particularly those entitlements that come directly from the federal government.

My formula for change will require some significant organizational restructuring. It will require reductions in spending. It will require dramatic tax reform and the repeal of two fatal Constitutional amendments. It will require legislative reform, enhancement and promotion of increased legal immigration, and a stop to illegal immigration and its associated programs. It will require the re-development of our manufacturing base, upgrading transportation, achieving environmentally stable energy independence, and building new cities. Our monetary supply system and our federal welfare programs will also require major overhauls.

Many don't really want to hear about or face up to these challenges. Some want to sweep them under the rug. Too many want to hide under the sheets and pretend our problems don't exist, and that drastic solutions are not required. Sometimes the challenges facing the country today band aid the inherent problems. The time of listening to political soothsayers proclaiming that "all is well" is over. Every citizen must recognize and accept this. I'm here to tell Americans that, yes, there will be pain and it's going to take hard work and sacrifice on everyone's part. However, skeptics might be surprised, even shocked, at how soon that pain will end if such changes are implemented thoroughly and expeditiously.

My belief is that the surest way to turn things around and change our failing tactics will be to allow ourselves to be guided by the Constitution. We must focus on those things that will bring about the cultural shifts to preserve the Constitutional principles established by our Founders and to make government serve in the way it was *meant* to serve. In order to lead this effort, my objective is to help Americans understand that these changes should not be viewed as a burden. In fact, it is our opportunity, and at its conclusion we will all feel thankful that we confronted these problems head on and "took the bull by the horns" before it was too late. We can and must perform this great work. The results will be something for which we will be forever proud, and something which our children and grandchildren will look back to and declare, "My parents did that. They pulled together and saved us. They saved the U.S. Constitution and our nation. They preserved for all of us the opportunities we enjoy today."

RESOLVE RATHER THAN REVOLVE

Our country needs problem solvers. There are too many who merely stir the pot. Such people are in a constant state of motion and commotion, stirring the pot and spinning the problems around and around, but never really resolving anything. At best they apply temporary Band-Aids. Many of the Band-Aid solutions grow to become part of the problem or grow into even bigger problems. Today's myopic politicians and bureaucrats create a climate where they *need* the problems to persist in order to justify their existence. In a desperate bid to preserve what they view as their own self-preservation, they quietly resist efforts to reduce government growth and implement common-sense solutions.

Because of this, we generally find ourselves back at the same place where we started. There's a reason human beings stranded in a vast desert are advised to use the sun and stars to guide their footsteps as they search for help. It's a natural tendency of the human body to place emphasis on either the right or left side of the body. Thus, the stranded survivor can end up walking in enormous circles and eventually arrive back where they started. It's the same with the system of problem-solving in American politics. Our elected officials—and even the voters themselves—end up walking in big circles. If the new generation learns nothing from the generation before, we continue to revolve around the same problems, hearing the same or similar arguments, but never really making any progress toward lasting solutions.

For more than a generation, we have tried to solve our problems by enacting more and more legislation requiring more and more money for more and more government programs. The unavoidable result is that more and more people become more and more dependent upon the government and doing less and less for themselves. People fail to recognize that the government and its programs are not healthy, nor do they have unlimited resources. They refuse to acknowledge that without real change and constitutional restraints, the system will surely fail. Unfortunately, there are too many who are more than happy to *watch* the system fail—even contributing to its demise. They want to establish something very different from the principles outlined by our Founding Fathers and the U.S. Constitution.

A SIMPLE SOLUTION

One of the ways in which bureaucrats or career politicians retain their position and continue to feather their nest is to repeat the mantra that solving these problems is infinitely complex. I'm here to proclaim that the solutions are amazingly simple. First and foremost, we must balance federal and state budgets, eliminate our national debt, and reduce our government to the "right size"—a *governable* size—and stop "taxation without limitation." This is the only way to remain free and rebuild a robust economy.

Bureaucrats will respond to such simple solutions with widened eyes and boldly declare that it can't be done. Or they'll simply dismiss such ideas as naive and simplistic. Here's the surprising irony: most common-sense thinkers will quickly acknowledge the wisdom of the solutions I've proposed, but will feel daunted and intimidated by the task of actually implementing them.

I boldly proclaim that the implementation is *not* much more complex than the solutions themselves. I believe like Pearl S. Buck: "The young do not know enough to be prudent, and therefore they attempt the impossible—and achieve it, generation after generation."

I'm here to present a simple and clear vision of the solutions to our nation's most pressing and intimidating problems. The path is straight and the vision is clear. It begins with acknowledging that all Americans are on the same side—Republicans and Democrats, conservatives and liberals, rich and poor, black and white, and every other class or distinction. These distinctions have too often been played against each other in an effort to keep problems alive and to prevent them from ever being solved. Those among us who truly wish to see America fail are a pitifully weak force compared to those who wish to see America prosper and triumph. Without a doubt, antagonistic voices can sound boisterously loud when they want to, but their clamors will be quickly dwarfed when those who wish to see America succeed make their voices heard.

As I unveil my platform and solutions for America's problems, it's generally expected that most will want to place my political vision inside some box for easy classification, whether Democrat or Republican, conservative or liberal, ultra-conservative or isolationist, Constitutionalist or Libertarian, or any number of other categories. It's human nature to try to categorize people—especially politicians—so they can either be dismissed out of hand or embraced by the like-minded.

I want to emphasize that the *label* is not as important as the *leadership*. Most intelligent leaders of any stripe can recognize solutions as a matter of common sense, but because they are immersed in our present party system and bureaucracy, they must remain beholden to certain forces and constituencies in order to retain power. This is the only way to guarantee their jobs, their status, and their reputations. In short, they must and will sacrifice principle and common sense for political influence and financial gain. Some of these individuals can no longer answer simple questions without feeling hemmed in by these various lobbies and constituents.

I might add that these lobbyists and special constituencies also have vested interests in keeping the status quo and do not want change because it upsets their balance of influence and benefits. Finally, there are some who have actually intertwined and entangled their own personal interests—whether financial, personal, or otherwise—within the very bureaucracies they help to create while serving in politics. This used to be called corruption, but because the associated legalese is also fed by burgeoning bureaucracies, few identify these entanglements by their proper terms.

This becomes the central argument for why America must elect a dark horse candidate like me for President. No representative, no senator, and no governor or state legislator should run for president while he or she is currently in office. They are being paid to serve, not to campaign. Nor should they serve for a period of time that defines such service as a career. Each should serve for a season and then return to the private sector.

The truth is, I love all people, and I can see the value and worth behind both sides of most arguments. Since I am not beholden to any constituency, party, or lobby, I can incorporate core principles of leadership to solve our problems more effectively than any long-time politician. I can and will lead this nation as a real statesman should.

It's been disappointing to watch so many civil servants ignore basic and fundamental principles of leadership and fail to solve problems and accomplish worthwhile objectives. Over the years I've developed many principles of leadership to guide my life. Many of these ideas came from other great leaders and entrepreneurs. I won't attempt to take credit or give credit for their origin. But the fact is, they *work*.

ESSENTIALS FOR LEADERSHIP

Leaders should be private, reflective, and encouraging. Leadership is not intimidation, coercion or creating conflict. Too many of today's politicians are too quick to try to win an argument by shaming and belittling their opponents. Some political pundits also participate in this practice. The vitriol generally expressed in this environment has not produced the desired results. The industry is trying to give their audiences what they think they want to hear. After all, it's a money-making venture and they all want to sell to their customers. Many say they would prefer a different tone of inclusion rather than division. However, it's difficult to burn bridges that you're trying to build. This is true for the President, and for every *candidate* for President.

Some may be disappointed that I don't make much effort to name names when it comes to expressing criticism. You won't find many instances—if any—where I pointedly call out individuals for incompetence or dishonesty. Yes, I disagree with many people and with their policies, but for the most part I recognize these policies as the offspring of circumstances. Nevertheless, I also acknowledge that each of us is individually responsible in some way. We must all accept accountability. I believe that most of these individuals sincerely believed, when certain policies were enacted, that they were doing the right thing. They probably ignored Constitutional principles because they felt they were smarter than the Founding Fathers or they didn't know the constitution. They may have wanted to see what the effects would be of certain social and political experiments. Again, this is why the Constitution is such an essential roadmap. By following it we have the best opportunity of avoiding serious errors and harmful experiments. This, and my faith in God, is what still gives me hope.

And now for the bright side. Because the primary infrastructure of the U.S. Constitution is still in place, we can still correct the mistakes that have been made before the United States deteriorates any further, before its principles become defunct, and before our freedoms are forfeited. I'm convinced that never in history has America gone more afield from its original founding ideologies. However, these mistakes can be corrected. Together we can make things right.

The objective of an effective leader must be to resolve the disconnects that exist and to promote goodwill, unity and teamwork. No one would deny that disconnects are rampant in America today. Never since the Civil War have Americans been so polarized. Some might be surprised at how swiftly our citizens could take sides or how another such great civil conflict could erupt. Some of deepest divides in our nation are between race, religion, wealth and power, resources and their availability, and who controls them. It would be downright foolish to deny that these are the very foundations of conflict and warfare since the beginning of time. It would be just as foolish to suppose that America is immune to such division or to ignore the fact that sudden violence could erupt in our streets that would quickly overwhelm a city or neighborhood and blaze out of control.

A leader must be clear and decisive. No one appreciates or wants a weather vane politician—a leader who is easily tossed and spun by every public whim or moralistic fashion. If you make a decision, you must stand by it. When you give direction to others, and then find that circumstances require a change of direction for whatever reason, don't blame others who have not caught up with your thinking. Be decisive and committed. Explain your reasons and move on. Also, far too much time is spent by "lost leaders" or rather "leaders who are lost" trying to cover their tracks in order to avoid future questions or criticism. Make good decisions that are based upon what is best now and in the future, not upon what people think or what you are *afraid* people will think.

A strong and great leader must be a problem solver and not a finger pointer. Finding fault or placing blame is never the solution. Placing blame only masks a problem, and may not show reality. Those who observe the finger pointers may conclude that they, *too,* will be blamed and criticized the next time. It encourages those serving around you to work below the line of effectiveness, efficiency and purposeful performance.

Someone described above-the-line-problem-solving to mean: "See it, own it, solve it, and do it." On the other hand, below-the-line (often called "blamestorming") means to ignore/deny, say "Hey, it's not *my* job," point fingers, promote confusion, cover your tail, and wait-and-see rather than offer solutions. Leaders must take full responsibility for their stewardship and for that for which they are responsible.

We can't blame the bureaucracy itself for all the mistakes. We *are* the bureaucracy, and if the system currently in place is not as efficient as it should be, then *we* must fix it. A great leader must find, utilize and be surrounded by the best wisdom and talent available. A great president takes responsibility for getting problems fixed and does it swiftly. Easier said than done? Perhaps. But generally not. Again, principle and common sense must prevail.

A leader must be a champion of growth and not a steward of stagnation. A leader must reject the bureaucrat mentality. We must not impose growth upon others. Big government dampens individual incentive and suppresses personal development. Continuous improvement is a personal and eternal principle. Even the United States of America must work within guidelines and systems that aid in the facilitation of each individual's freedom to grow and work in order to progress.

A leader must be a source of strength and not a perpetuator of fear. For America to be strong it must not allow fear to dominate the public mind. Nor can we show fear to our enemies. Lastly, fear cannot be entertained in the minds of those who *serve* with a president. A president, often unknowingly, surrounds himself with yes-men simply because of his weakness as a leader. This can create a climate where subordinates are afraid of being questioned or accused. In such an atmosphere, people will manipulate facts or information. Over time, the organization can destroy itself.

When people operate in a culture of fear it stifles ingenuity and feedback. People say and do only what is expected, accepted or what is politically correct. They might go silent and no longer make meaningful contributions. They will move away if they are not already being nudged out by the powers that surround them. If a president cannot inspire the best from those around him, solutions will never be achieved, stagnation will be the general outcome, and bureaucracies will continue to grow.

These are foundational rules associated with fundamental leadership itself. Yet, it's been alarming how readily such ideas have been ignored by those in our highest offices of trust.

BUILD ON STRENGTHS

A leader must build on strengths, not accentuate weaknesses. We all have weaknesses. To focus on or exploit those weaknesses demonstrates insecurity and fear. Leaders can overcome their own weaknesses by implementing correct principles of leadership. It's very difficult, if not impossible, for individuals to overcome their weaknesses when that is all that others see or focus on. Pulling others down does not promote growth or progress. However, the opposite is powerful. Building up and supporting those around us will promote both growth and progress while developing good will. How often do we hear gratitude or congratulations expressed between politicians, particularly those of different political parties? Such courtesies are far too rare.

POLITICS AS USUAL

Many campaigners for political office have pledged to work "across the aisle" for the greater good of the nation. Yet after the election they fail miserably to do so. Some elected officials arrive in Washington bright-eyed with anticipation, fully intending to make a difference, but then find themselves caught up in the petty bureaucratic "politics as usual" that have been allowed to infect these institutions for far too long. Again, common sense can resolve these problems, but it is often futile and illogical to expect the institutions themselves or the professional politicians to make the necessary changes.

Which congressional body, for example, would vote for itself to accept a decrease in benefits or pay? Which body would vote itself out of a job by incorporating term limits? Against the intent of our Founders, too many modern politicians find themselves immersed in continuous campaigning and the realities of a 24-hour news cycle. Such a world forces them to devote an increasingly significant block of time and resources simply to holding onto their jobs. I'm not necessarily advocating term limits, but it is one means of insuring that elected officials remain statesmen—men and women whose motives for making a difference are pure and *stay* pure while weeding out those who intend to make politics a career. Some may fully intend, after a period of service, to return to the private life they left behind. The argument often made by politicians, especially those who have served for long periods, is that to better serve their constituencies they must retain seniority in established traditions of power and seniority in both congressional houses. This argument illustrates why certain problems continue to recycle and are never solved.

The problem of career politicians who no longer serve the voters is undeniable. Perhaps there are other solutions besides term limits, but few in leadership positions are seriously striving to find them. A true leader will be disciplined and demand that such a foundational problem is solved *first*, understanding that the solutions to *other* problems will quickly follow.

I'm committed to this resolve and will show it by not campaigning for a second term of office. If the people of the United States of America like what I do as their president, I will serve them again, but I will not waste my time nor your valuable resources for an exhaustive and expensive second campaign.

COMING TOGETHER—THIS TIME FOR REAL

So many candidates and politicians have promised to heal that which divides us. I fear the public now just rolls their eyes in disbelief and disgust. In fact, many have already decided that the prospect of unity is no longer feasible, and therefore they've entrenched themselves behind one line or another—unbendable, intransigent, and uncompromising. This may be the most unfortunate—and dangerous—reality that exists in America today.

Never has there been so much resentment and hostility shown by candidates toward other candidates. As a result, America finds itself divided and galvanized against its own future. Nowhere is this culture more apparent than in political campaigns. Candidates and their supporters consider other candidates to be their enemy, and they look only to attack the other candidates' weaknesses in order to defeat and destroy them.

The very nature of my personality is to reject this approach. Because I feel too much respect even for those who differ in opinion from my own, and because I genuinely feel even those who disagree with me can make valuable contributions to the betterment of America, I will not, during my campaign for President of the United States, resort to negative campaigning. I may criticize policies, strategies, philosophies, and bureaucracies, but I will not engage in personal attacks against other candidates.

I am told that countless studies have been conducted by various pundits and pollsters that negative campaigning is actually an effective tool for defeating one's opponent. They repeat the philosophy that negativity *works*. They promote the notion that shaping public perception against another candidate in a way that is vilifying and degrading has proven again and again to be a winning strategy. I don't care about such studies. I reject that approach. I understand that candidates can gain an advantage by pandering to the baser instincts of human beings. I simply refuse to play that game. I cannot and will not do this because it goes against everything I believe in as a patriot, as a Christian, and as a member of the human race. Far too many politicians, it seems, have sold their souls for a job in public service by behaving in a manner that contradicts their conscience and their nature. This is sad and destructive to everyone. It is not necessary. We can do better and *be* better than this.

Sometimes secondary voices, such as Political Action Committees (PACS), are the ones who support their candidates by making vitriolic attacks against the other candidates. Often a candidate has no control over this approach, but afterwards they make only a token effort to correct the attack or discourage such activities. In my campaign, such mudslinging will not be tolerated. The position I take, and the swift and sharp response I make against those who vilify other candidates may even offend my own supporters. Yet to support my candidacy means first and foremost that you must support my philosophy of campaigning, which is one of persuasion and unification, not division. My campaign must be one of building and repairing bridges. We must teach, inspire and include. Attacking and vilifying others alienates potential voters from wanting to vote more than it inspires them. Let us individually and as a nation be respectful, tolerant and appealing. I have to believe that truth and reason *will* win the day or there is no point in campaigning to save the United States of America. The time of widening the gaps that presently exist must end. America must finally come together.

Thus, I openly and vehemently dismiss the sentiments of pundits and pollsters who proclaim that negative campaigning—attacking other candidates in a way that is personal and degrading—is the only way to win. Our conscience and my soul are more important than winning; more important than fame, fortune, power or any other accolade. The truth is, if candidates must compromise such convictions to become the President of the United States, then they do not deserve the job.

That declaration, I hope, represents the profile of a true leader. I invite all Americans and all other candidates to join with me in leading America in this manner. Let us do it with respect, with dignity and with patience. Sometimes the best reaction is no reaction.

Chapter 11

Policies of Goverment, Peace, and War

DIGGING OUT

Few would contest the fact that our present problems in America have placed us on a dangerous and declining path that is both unsustainable and going in the wrong direction. I sought an analogy from my personal life that would best illustrate this point. We've all watched on television or read in the news some heart-wrenching stories about digging out after blizzards, hurricanes, and earthquakes and finding a brighter day on the horizon.

Then I recalled one of my first major jobs as a young man, helping the Chapman family in Groveland, Idaho, a small town near where I grew up. I love the Chapman family, and they have expressed great love for me. They operated a family dairy farm, along with raising other cash crops. I was fifteen years old, almost six feet tall, and could work all day as long as I was properly fed. In the summers I hauled hay, built fences and dug ditches. In the fall I bucked sacks of potatoes and emptied them into the spud (potato) cellars. It was actually the Chapman's ten-year-old twins, Deon and Cleon, who taught me how to back a tractor and trailer into their spud cellar. One of my favorite memories was having unrestricted access to their milk barn and an open invitation to drink all the fresh chilled milk that I could drink from the huge stainless steel holding tank with an available ladle.

One spring, after a harsh winter, the temperatures rose quickly. Everything thawed out, and pastures were already turning green. Mr. Chapman seemed almost embarrassed as he pointed to his corral gate that opened inward. He explained that during a harsh blizzard, he had not let the herd of Holstein cows out to the pasture for a long time. He had just fed them in the corral and spread straw to keep them clean. The manure level piled up higher and higher, and then the gate froze solid, so he couldn't open it. He continued to feed the herd in the corral for the rest of the winter. Now that everything was thawing out, the cows were wading in a two-foot-deep pool of green, soupy manure. It was a mess getting them ready to milk twice a day.

Mr. Chapman was running out of feed and needed to get his herd out of that corral and into the pasture. He humbly shook his head in apology and said, lowering his voice so that his twins couldn't hear, "Dale, as you can see, we are in deep (he paused and slowly spelled out the word)—D U N G. We really need your help." He then offered me a pair of hip wading boots, a manure fork, scoop shovel, and a clean pair of rubber gloves.

I donned the boots and gloves, climbed over the fence, and waded into the soupy morass up to my knees and went to work. At times, I thought I wasn't making any progress. The odor was terrible and sometimes overpowering. Occasionally I opened up a pocket of ammonia fumes from the midst of the sludge. It burned my nose and made my eyes water. I finally got the gate open, the cows out to the pasture, and the tractor bucket in to do the rest of the cleanup. The work was hard and time-consuming, but I got the job done.

From this story, I hope you can glean the comparison I'm trying to make with the circumstances in which we Americans find ourselves now. In this case Mr. Chapman was fully aware that he had made some errors. He was even humble about the way he expressed these facts to me. But the problem still existed and had to be fixed. I accepted the job because I loved the Chapman family and he was my employer. The situation is remarkably similar for the United States of America. I love this country. Because of the freedoms, liberties and opportunities it has provided for my life, I believe this nation also loves me. We may not yet be in over our heads with D U N G, but metaphorically we are certainly in it up to our knees, and we need to get to work and dig our way out.

AN ORGANIZATIONAL RESTRUCTURING

We have a fundamental need to follow the Constitution. This is difficult to do in an environment where proven principles of leadership are not employed. Leadership principles are understood and employed by everyone from the CEOs of Fortune 500 Companies to a humble scout master guiding his half dozen boys. Moreover, the principles of leadership works very well in building strong families. They ought to be preached, utilized, and mastered for this reason alone. We must create a political climate of trust and respect, working in an environment where members of the House and the Senate and leaders of *all* the governmental departments are committed— *actually* committed—to transforming our current federal government into that which would best serve the American people. But where do we begin? What tools do we need, and where do we start digging?

The answer is common sense. We begin with the hardest, messiest job first—the circumstances which might be best compared to the situation I've already described with Mr. Chapman and his cows. So what is that job? It's the organizational restructuring of our government on a federal and legislative level to correct the mistakes that allowed big government to get out of control. This is what we must clean up so we can open the gate and get in to clean up the rest of the corral.

Now we can get into some of the specifics of my platform—the "beef"—as some old commercials for fast-food hamburgers used to say. It finally allows readers and pundits to begin to analyze my statements to decide which category of the political spectrum I might fall in. So be it. Let the punditry begin. In the end, however, I hope that everyone will realize, when it comes to issues of solving our most pressing problems, there's far more common ground than anyone might suspect. It's hard work and it's messy. Sometimes we'll wonder if we're making progress because corruption, waste, and inefficiency stink like D U N G – and it's hard to get rid of. But it *can be done!*

CONGRESSIONAL REFORM

I have a conviction that serving as an elected official, as well as serving as President, should be considered an honor and act of service, not a career. The Founding Fathers envisioned *citizen* legislators and presidents. The attitude of all senators and congressmen should be that they serve their term(s), and then go home and get back to doing what they were doing before they sought political office. George Washington was not a professional politician. He was the person who everyone could trust to guide them in this great experiment. In a symbolic and perhaps remote way, he was the Founders' "dark horse candidate." Many historians have noted that if George Washington had desired to be America's first king, many citizens in the colonies would have supported him. We can thank God that one of the most ardent supporters of that sacred document created in Philadelphia a few years earlier was George Washington.

The quickest and most reasonable way to restructure our present federal government is by aiming at the politicians' pocketbooks. Congressmen, senators, the president and vice president, cabinet members, etc., should indeed be paid a salary for their work while in office. But, they should not be paid for not working or for campaigning. At the conclusion of their service perhaps they should also receive a modest, short-term severance. But that's it. End of story. After six months, or at most a year, any salary or benefits associated with the office must end. No life pensions, no long-term health benefits, and no other financial advantages whatsoever. Why would citizens (their employers) agree to pay them when they are not working or long after they leave their jobs? Citizens have not agreed to this. The professional politicians have given this to themselves.

All of these executives (past, present and future) should participate in putting money into our current Social Security system, just as they did in private life. Politicians should have to purchase and develop their own personal retirement plans, the same as all other Americans. Executives should no longer have the exclusive power to vote themselves a pay raise or give themselves additional benefits. Congressional pay should only rise annually as outlined by a measurable algorithm, such as the lower of a Consumer Price Index (CPI) or 3% increase, or whatever coincides with the fluctuating changes of the national economy. If the economy is going down, so should the salaries of public servants and government employees.

Like any other organization, congressional offices should have health insurance and other benefits available to its participants while performing their jobs. But after a politician's term has concluded, these individuals should participate in the same health care system as other Americans. It's critical to our constitutional republic that our public servants abide by the same laws imposed upon all other American citizens. We must prevent the creation of an elitist class with expectations that taxpayers will support them for the rest of their lives. We should not have incentives for seeking office beyond the desire to work hard and serve the voters who put them into office. Such rules should be enacted to include all past and present public servants and employees. The enticing and corrupted perks of holding office must be eliminated and rendered null and void.

Since the Second World War the number of employees for the federal government has exploded. Fear of the Cold War and a desire to stimulate the economy was the "severe blizzard" that caused Americans to allow government to grow out of control. The Cold War as it was defined in the eighties may be over, and the "pastures are now green," but the federal government is full of stinking and sloppy D U N G. It's clear that no one has had the courage to declare "no more," to put on the hip waders and gloves and to shovel us out in order to open the gate.

You might remember that when President Harry Truman "retired from office in 1952, his income was a U.S. Army pension reported to have been $13,507.72 a year. It's time to cut back. As President, I will personally and symbolically place a fifty percent (50 percent) cut on my presidential paycheck. I will eliminate many of the perks I have identified so those funds can go back into federal coffers to help pay off our national debt and keep it from coming back! Congress, noting that he was paying for his stamps and personally licking them, granted him an 'allowance' and later, a retroactive pension of $25,000 per year. After President Eisenhower was inaugurated, Harry and Bess drove home to Missouri by themselves. There was no Secret Service following them."

Can we not expect the same character in the President of the United States today?

Many federal government departments created in previous decades have not proven their worth or lived up to their promise—or even their practical purpose. They've become institutions that demand more taxation without limitation and produce only stagnation. There are many departments and agencies that have produced no measurable improvement in the quality of service or quality of life for Americans. Yet billions upon billions of dollars continue to be poured into federally directed programs that should have been the states' responsibilities.

The result has often been to suffocate innovation and problem solving on the local level with increased bureaucracy and paperwork. The best interest of the states and of American citizens has been buried under thousands of additional paper pushers who launch new program after new program. From a great and disconnected distance, the bureaucrats in Washington first measure a problem, then attempt to fix it, then implement the fixes, and finally measure and see if the fixes had any impact. In the final analysis the government itself becomes the problem while the status quo remains relatively unchanged. Such bureaucracies have become burdened with buildings and offices and multitudes of employees managing programs instead of serving people.

When have we last heard of a politician successfully eliminating a federal agency? Those who would attempt, for example, to say that a government department or agency is ultimately ineffective, and even damaging toward the institution it seeks to improve, are accused of being heartless and uncaring of the people or the country. They are often shouted into submission by aggressive and demanding voices.

This negative campaign of emotional manipulation has been extraordinarily effective for generations in preserving and defending government bureaucracy. It is now supported in an age of twenty-four-hour news, where the most sensational accusations receive much of the attention.

Lest I be misunderstood, I'm not saying that all departments and agencies of the government should be abolished, or that even the ones I perceive as burdensome should be eliminated overnight. A hiring freeze should be immediately implemented. Attrition and reassignment are healthy strategies for shrinking a bloated bureaucracy. Some agencies should be combined. Honest evaluation and bold initiatives will allow changes to be implemented. Some departments and agencies should be gradually defunded, with their obligations and responsibilities being transferred back to states. Often these responsibilities can even be delegated to local jurisdictions. We must empower those who are closest to a problem the opportunity of finding real, lasting solutions. It's generally necessary to get close to a problem, smell the stink, and get a little dirty in order to solve it. You can't do it from a distance!

Unfortunately, many have come to believe that the federal government should oversee practically everything. This is the path to socialism. Actually, it is socialism, not a democratic republic, that promotes a cradle-to-grave nanny state whose objective is to ensure that its citizens are never lacking in anything. Yet this attitude is very different—almost embarrassingly so—from the vision that our Founding Fathers intended.

As soon as I am elected, I will propose the aforementioned hiring freeze upon the federal workforce and manage a steady reduction by attrition and prudent reassignments as needed. I would also push for an immediate ten percent (10 percent) cut in the Congressional budget and eliminate perks and lifetime pensions. Many of the responsibilities currently usurped by the federal government must be placed back into the hands of the states. This can only be accomplished by repealing the 16th and 17th Amendments to the U.S. Constitution.

The current economic climate would also demand that we cease most foreign aid; particularly military aid that supports questionable allies. I would work toward having government-funded museums and national parks pay for themselves through tourism, private donations and volunteer support. Users, in general, should be willing to accept a bigger share of costs for public services.

See what I mean? I already mentioned that Americans would experience some sacrifice and some pain. Some of these ideas will cause some jaws to drop in alarm. Many will insist that these programs cost only a trifle or a pittance and must be preserved at any cost. Again, we return to the issue of trust. Americans must trust that I also have a deep and abiding love for American landmarks and institutions. But the institution and republic called the United States of America must come first. We will leave no stone unturned and analyze every expense, and when added up together, the savings will total far more than a pittance or a trifle. Some costs intertwined and inbred into the bureaucracy will add up to significant costs indeed.

Please note that I'm not proposing a reckless slashing of agencies and programs that will put tens of thousands of people suddenly out of work. Every change must be carefully assessed, common sense must guide our actions, but solutions must be employed. Most people are willing to make sacrifices for the common good—that is, until it's spelled out how such sacrifices will directly affect *them*. The objective will be to have sacrifices made across the board so that all Americans from every income level can play a role in saving our country.

NATIONAL DEFENSE

I'm a strong believer in having a superior, well-prepared, and well-trained and equipped military. America should be second to none when it comes to our capacity to defend ourselves and our interests when they come under threat. However, the fact is that the United States has become entangled in numerous conflicts throughout the world where we never should have become involved. These have cost billions of dollars, to say nothing of the precious cost of human lives. Even in times of relative peace, I believe an argument can be made that our foreign policy has too often caused waste, unnecessary bureaucracy, and dangerously ineffective interventions. The point is that the entire intelligence community and Defense Department must be re-evaluated and reorganized in order to preserve the United States and the ideas upon which it was founded.

Such an overhaul should take place no matter what the current circumstances of our economy. But, in the face of the massive debt that threatens to undermine our sovereignty, as well as the individual freedoms of the citizens, such an overhaul has become more important than perhaps at any other time in our history. Honestly, every politician in history likes to use this kind of rhetoric—proclaiming that a situation has never been more dire than it is right now—but in the case of the current burdens we face with regard to our national debt and its relationship to so many other facets of our economy, I fear this is one of the those times when the statement is frighteningly accurate.

While I would support strengthening our military in certain ways to keep our nation safe, I would simultaneously and carefully measure our current military involvement overseas. This would be a very thoughtful process involving the finest military minds. We must be far more selective in foreign deployment and the kinds of conflicts in which we are willing to become engaged. In today's world economy and international political landscape, we cannot afford to be the planet's policemen. Nations must be responsible for their own security and that of their neighbors. They cannot expect the United States to solve all of their problems. We must clearly define and justify our national interests and not fall into the trap of perpetual conflict.

The one exception is to act in cases where military involvement protects our independence and sovereignty as a nation. The majority of the conflicts since World War II have resulted in a terrible cost of American lives, goodwill and economic resources. Other nations must be allowed to resolve their own problems without our interference. Too often, our interference creates a bigger problem than the one we went in to fix. Our military should not be used to provide aid to foreign nations or to fix their internal problems. Its purpose is to fight and win wars in order to protect the United States from foreign aggression.

Certainly in many of these foreign conflicts there are despicable villains and there are severely oppressed peoples, but there may be little justification for the United States to unilaterally take sides. When we do, we provoke the hatred of the rising generation and inflict a wound that can fester until it splits wide open, forcing Americans into yet another conflict. Here, it appears, America has learned little from the lessons of World War I—a conflict wherein neither side—Allies or Axis—had a particularly lofty moral justification for their aggressions, but where most alliances were drawn for political reasons. It was, however, the brutal peace treaty of Versailles following World War I—a harsh agreement of punishment and reparations that America supported and helped to install—that led to the bitter hatred and passion for revenge that eventually became the Third Reich.

Every time we hear barking around the world, it doesn't mean we need to kill the dog. By the same token, just because there's a storm brewing in some other region of the globe, we don't need to act like weather gods who can make the storm go away. Sometimes nature must take its course, no matter how devastating and destructive. This doesn't mean we ignore such storms or the barks of certain vicious dogs, but I believe in following the U.S. Constitution and focusing on defense instead of aggression. A moderate exercise of caution might lead to far more positive outcomes. Again, if we're speaking in terms of history, this is merely the worst kind of Monday morning quarterbacking. But if we're talking about the future, many of these ideas must be adopted. We shouldn't perpetually mourn the mistakes of the past, but we can learn from them and develop policies that demonstrate what we have learned.

My effort as President will be to exhaust every alternative that keeps the United States out of war. However, if American interests and American security are truly at risk, we cannot capitulate as a nation and cower in the face of danger. If our very safety and freedom is at stake, we must act decisively to use the necessary force of our military capabilities.

In the event of such clear and present danger and with an overwhelming congressional approval of a declaration of war, every aspect of society must unite. If we are going to war, then we will go together and fight until we are victorious. Any dissenters, including careless media coverage and propaganda, must be reined in – think about it – during war. This must include gossiping politicians and other sources who reveal military strategies or events before they are executed and authorized for release. Such carelessness has too often directly resulted in greater loss of American life and making missions more difficult.

War, by its ugliest and most brutal definition, is the last option to problem resolution. Warfare and its images were never meant as entertainment for the American public or world audiences. Nor should the media be broadcasting elements of its reality day after day, hour after hour, and often minute by minute. Stories and images from the battlefront should not be manipulated or used as tools of propaganda that damage or weaken our military advantage or civilian resolve. When engaging in warfare, secrecy and discretion must be considered matters of paramount importance to insure its successful execution. Under my leadership we will not be drawn into ambiguous police or peace-keeping actions. When war is declared, we will all go to war with a clear victory as our goal.

Trust is always vital. In such sober and serious situations, Americans must have confidence and trust in their leaders. If I might paraphrase Ronald Reagan: "Trust with *verification* and *clarification*." It must be clearly defined how the military war effort will be implemented and what conditions and restrictions will be imposed until the conflict is over. These are very serious matters, but they are not complex. It all comes back to reason, discipline and common sense. We must insist that government be limited to doing what it was meant to do. This will allow individuals, groups and organizations to offer the compassionate service that they should be free to offer.

Chapter 12

Losing Our Way

GETTING AT THE ROOTS OF THE PROBLEM

In my youth, still trying to comprehend the ways of the world, I remember listening to my father talk politics with neighbors over the fence, on the street corner, and in the field. They'd bemoan such things as Social Security and the Internal Revenue Service. What strikes me as unusual today is that these discussions didn't really trumpet a personal disgust with taxes or "the system." They always related to how my family and neighbors felt these laws were hurting individuals and the population as a whole.

I have siblings and their spouses who are quite savvy and consistently alert on issues of politics. Through childhood and beyond, I remember long discussions about America and the best ways to solve our problems. As with any young man, my first political impressions or leanings were influenced heavily by those closest to me. Then, as time went on and as I studied, traveled overseas, served, and met many wonderful people from every race and religion, age and financial status, these perspectives were honed and deepened. This occurred most dramatically at Boston College in the early '70s, where so many of the people I met came from entirely different backgrounds and political viewpoints. It was an era where many voices dramatically expressed vehemence against the government. Our nation seemed on the verge of revolution—quite literally. I felt compelled to decide where I stood on practically every issue. As the country became galvanized against the Viet Nam War, and as the drug culture started to expand, a general feeling of "Down with the establishment!" echoed among my classmates. Perhaps I should have felt surprised at how little I was personally influenced by these sentiments. Instead of allowing myself to be swept up in the hue and cry of the anti-establishment, I still felt deeply patriotic. I loved America and had no hesitation about expressing those feelings whenever the setting called for it. After studying history, politics, and the Constitution I would strive to sharpen my political viewpoints, and on occasion even alter them to form opinions that differed from those held by the people who had influenced me in my youth.

What surprises many people that I've spoken to over the years is my ability to find ideas and wisdom in many sources. Politics has a way of galvanizing people into rigid categories of thinking. For some reason I could never quite fit wholly into any one political mold or party. On the most part, I've voted Republican, and yet I have disagreed with some party practices. I've come to understand that there is no one and only true political party. Each party has good ideas and worthy candidates. Americans must look for the best and leave the rest.

My interest has always been to simply do what's right— listening to my conscience rather than allowing myself to be manipulated by loud, clever or soothing rhetoric. In general, all people claim to have the same innate ability, but it's been my observation that they really don't. Most choose to be followers and their first inclination is to align themselves with those whose established opinions match their own. Fortunately, in my life I've found I could develop close relationships with just about anyone.

BILL BRADLEY

During my senior year at London Central High School in England, I had a chance to meet my greatest hero at that time in my life. Bill Bradley had helped win the Olympic gold medal for the United States in basketball in 1964. He was the NCAA Player of the Year in 1965. He turned down many offers to play professionally in order to attend Oxford University as a Rhodes Scholar. He would later play for the New York Knicks for ten years and help carry them to two championship titles. As fate would have it, he was the commencement speaker at my high school graduation in the spring of 1966.

Keep in mind, at this time in my life sports made up my entire world. During the graduation ceremony I sat right behind him on the stage. I reached out to touch his arm, perhaps hoping that some of the magic would rub off on me. It did, as he spoke to the audience about doing our best and becoming all we can be to bring out the greatness within each of us. After his inspiring address, I had the privilege of helping to drive him (with my friend Buff Blount who is now a retired Army General) back to his apartment at nearby Oxford University. Bradley invited us in. He seemed mature beyond his years. I have vivid memories of him serving us refreshments and taking the time to share valuable nuggets of wisdom that have influenced me ever since.

Bill Bradley also ran successfully for two terms as a United States Senator from New Jersey and even tried unsuccessfully to win the Democratic nomination for President in 2000. Even then, I was fully aware that he held some political views that were in conflict with my own, but there were other areas where we stood in full agreement. In any case, I gained incredible respect for the manner in which he conducted himself and his efforts to honestly weigh both sides of an issue before adopting a position. As I later watched his future successes unfold, he served as an example and a testimonial that a sports hero could become so much more. I learned by his example and the examples of many others as I sought to make my own mark in the world.

The truth is that I genuinely love people and I can empathize with folks from every walk of life. I've benefited tremendously from this gift as I've raised my family, worked in business, and served others. The intuitive respect that I've felt for different cultures has never waned as I have had wonderful opportunities to live in various parts of the world.

Just because I say this, don't make the mistake of judging me as being ambivalent or equivocal about the most important issues that affect our lives. When it comes to solving problems, my solutions will likely take a very different tack from what most others might suggest. My objective is to focus upon the very root of why a problem persists or why it crops up again in other forms. The roots of our nation's most serious problems, I believe, are in the lowered standards and level of moral integrity among Americans and getting away from the Constitution.

THE SEEDS OF DISENFRANCHISEMENT

Some Constitutional amendments clarify and enhance personal freedoms while others were designed specifically to give the government more power. The former should be retained and the latter repealed. In particular, I would like to consider here the 16th and 17th Amendments. In order to understand the subtle nature of the imbalances, inefficiencies, and dangers introduced by these amendments we need to understand the entire process by which the Constitution was conceived, written, and ratified. The introspection and intellectual debate behind the Constitution may be one of the most misunderstood and underappreciated achievements in our exceptional history. Each American citizen should read and study the Constitution to be reminded that the careful checks and balances forged into this inspired document grew from some of the most extraordinary human reflection.

Its framers relied upon observations of virtually every existing government and legislature of Europe, including those that were extinct, carefully perusing the works of philosophical giants of the Renaissance as well ancient intellectuals such as Socrates, Plato and Aristotle. The Constitution was written as much for our time and the future as it was for theirs. The Founding Fathers studied, compared and mulled over republics and democracies from history, trying to discover why they succeeded and why they ultimately failed. The Constitution's framers were rightfully obsessed with how to institute the best form of government—one that would identify the frailties of human nature, check government force, prevent corruption, and keep ambition in check. The object was to circumscribe the affairs of men by the rule of law in such a way as to bring out the better attributes of our nature, reward innovation, and tear down any obstacle that might prevent the common person from achieving greatness.

Today's students, at many levels of our educational system, should be required to study not only the text of the Constitution, but also works such as *The Federalist Papers* by Alexander Hamilton and James Madison. These papers would help students develop an understanding of the reasoning and rationale behind each of the Constitution's articles. I believe, if this were done, the average American would easily recognize the inherent dangers of the 16th and 17th Amendments— dangers so subtle, so cunning, and yet so destructive that it has taken a full century for the infection to fully work its way into the system. We are now seeing these destructive forces in daily manifestations of crisis.

For some people this might be a difficult concept to comprehend and accept. After all, wasn't it during the last century that the United States fought and won two world wars, weathered the Great Depression, and rose to prominence as the most powerful and prosperous nation on earth? It is important to realize that America rose to prominence on the world stage for numerous reasons. Its prominence was built on the underpinnings of innovation laid down in the nineteenth century, a status to be fully realized in the twentieth century.

The 16th and 17th Amendments were both ratified in 1913. In this year the House, the Senate, and the Presidency were all controlled by one party. The nation itself was very much in a volatile, optimistic mood. Our first socialist congressmen had been elected to office, and new movements of progressivism and populism were sweeping the country. This was coupled with the ambitions of many for expanding the power and wealth of the federal government and building up the U.S. military so it could compete with the increasingly technologically advanced militaries of Europe, Great Britain, and Japan. The legislatures of the various states, facing intense pressure from the media (sound familiar?) and other pressures from the federal government, ignored basic founding principles and allowed two new amendments to supersede and abolish several of the original Constitutional clauses that had been carefully laid down and secured in place by our Founding Fathers.

THE 16TH AMENDMENT

Prior to 1913 the principles outlined by the Constitution for the federal government to collect taxes could be found primarily in a number of clauses, beginning with Article I, Section 2, Clause 3:

Representatives and direct Taxes shall be apportioned among the several States which may be included within this Union, according to their respective Numbers . . .

Included with this was Article I, Section 8, Clause 1:

The Congress shall have Power to lay and collect Taxes, Duties, Imposts and Excises, to pay the Debts and provide for the common Defence and general Welfare of the United States; but all Duties, Imposts and Excises shall be uniform throughout the United States.

And finally Article I, Section 9, Clause 4:

No Capitation, or other direct, Tax shall be laid, unless in proportion to the Census or Enumeration herein before directed to be taken.

These clauses insured that taxes to support the federal government were provided by the individual states. Some people today may have been taught that the idea of a universal income tax had never been considered prior to 1913. In truth, it was imposed during the War of 1812 and the Civil War. In other words, it had been used in times of emergency, when the federal government needed funds for special and temporary reasons. Otherwise, the primary sources of federal revenue from the Constitutional Convention until 1913 came from customs, duties and excise taxes paid for by the states. This all ended in 1913 when these forms of collecting revenue were superseded by a singular, brief, and overwhelming sentence known as the 16th Amendment. It reads as follows:

The Congress shall have power to lay and collect taxes on incomes, from whatever source derived, without apportionment among the several States, and without regard to any census or enumeration.

"Taxation without representation" was ended by the Declaration of Independence, but "taxation without limitation" began with the 16th Amendment. The very idea that these thirty words passed the scrutiny of the American populace— with such a long tradition of rejecting unjust taxes, accepting these sweeping, unbridled powers of taxation—is shocking. Citizens just let it happen. America's vision was clouded by the ambitions of several progressive presidents at the turn of the twentieth century. Such leaders in the Presidency and in Congress desired to expand the powers of the federal government in a global race to first keep up with and then stay ahead of other countries. Whether the reasons were just or unjust, the individual states literally sacrificed their own ability to accept or reject the money-raising demands of Uncle Sam. The checks and balances incorporated to protect against just such abuses were abolished, seemingly overnight. The power of the states devolved into a status of legislative insignificance. This was never the intent of our Founding Fathers. They did then, and would have now, vehemently fought against such changes.

In the beginning, the National Federal Income Tax was relatively small, but because the amendment was unlimited in scope and unchecked by any other clause of the Constitution, it was inevitable that it would soon be abused. We see the results of those abuses today—abuses that can be wielded against specific parties, income brackets, political factions, and even specific individuals. Without this amendment many of the tax laws related to the New Deal, Social Security, and the funding of many other government departments and agencies would not have been possible. This includes, most recently, the program of "taxation" (as defined by the Supreme Court) known as the Affordable Care Act, or Obamacare. Without the 16th Amendment this act would not have been possible. Such programs and their governing bureaucracies would have been left to the individual states and localities who best understood the needs of the people living there. This is precisely where our Founding Fathers repeatedly stated that such powers should remain.

One single sentence—that's all it took. One sentence stripped the authority of the states to serve as a buffer against this type of federal overreach for all time. Unless—and this is an enormous "unless"—America can somehow be convinced of this great error and repeal this amendment, we will have forever lost the natural checks and balances of our republic.

One might ask, "Are you serious? One sentence? Did the three branches of government and the legislatures of two-thirds of the states in 1913 really think such a complex issue as collecting taxes from all its citizens could be encapsulated in a single sentence?" That's precisely what I'm saying. I'm all for brevity when it comes to establishing sound principles, but here is an example where a single sentence—thirty words—has caused more pain, bureaucracy, corruption and debt than any other sentence in the history of American lawmaking. The solution would be as simple as the following amendment: *"The 16th Amendment is hereby repealed."* Six words and we would be getting back on the right path.

Some might respond, "But hey, I *like* the benefits we receive from some of these social programs made possible by the 16th Amendment, including Social Security and Obamacare." This is the usual response, especially of politicians who support this amendment, but the fact is that such a response entirely misses the most essential point. There's no denying that some of these programs, because of how they are managed, are so bloated with bureaucracy as to enlarge the very problems they were established to solve. The real problem is not the objectives of these programs. It's who controls them. The intention of our Founders was that they should be placed in the hands of local states and municipalities. Instead, they are in the hands of the federal government.

The result is that a federal program like Social Security has become so embedded in our psyche that the very notion of an America without it seems frightening. We envision our streets suddenly overrun with starvation, exposure, and violence. My argument is—and has always been—that individual responsibility cannot be legislated away by federal law. The individual states and municipalities are in a better position to assess and administer the solutions to their own problems without interference from the federal government.

After all we've learned from history, who could possibly disagree? Again, the key is to employ common sense. What American, for the last one hundred years, could deny the waste of billions of dollars misspent by Washington, D.C., trying to implement and enforce the compounding number of federal programs? The Internal Revenue Service has developed into a massive regulatory industry and an intimidating force. It continues to grow with voluminous regulations and penalties.

Some might argue, "How can we trust the states or localities to take care of all these social needs?" The problem is that we've become so accustomed to letting the federal government control these matters that many don't even consider a better way—the Constitutional way. The states and municipalities could, and would, do a far better job.

What we've forgotten is that our Founding Fathers specifically sought to protect the citizens of this country against such federal overreach. And the logic is undeniable. Again, let's consider reason. Does it make more sense to handle such issues on a local level, where local leaders can personally observe and listen to the constituencies of that locality, or to place such programs in the hands of disassociated bureaucrats in Washington? The framers of the Constitution understood this, and fought with all their might to establish principles that would protect the Union from such disassociation and to keep the federal government in check.

I've grown up watching and waiting for our leaders to solve these problems. I don't see anyone else doing it. It's time for a president to rally the American people and their elected representatives to solve this problem once and for all. I'm prepared. I'm ready, and I will do my part.

THE 17TH AMENDMENT

The history of the 17th Amendment and the factors that brought it to pass are interesting indeed. Most Americans take for granted that senators are chosen by popular vote. They are not even vaguely aware that senators were ever selected differently, and very few could explain the original thinking of the Founding Fathers as to why such individuals should be chosen by state legislatures.

The fact is that in 1913—the same year and just months after the passage of the 16th Amendment—this essential and vital power of state government was stripped away and handed over to the general populace. Some might wonder, how can that be a bad thing? Why *shouldn't* senators—in fact why shouldn't *all* public servants—be directly elected by the people?

To understand why the election of senators and congressmen should be different, we must examine the rationale of the Framers who gave us the Constitution. The original system of having congressmen chosen by popular vote while having senators chosen by state legislatures was a very sensitive issue for them. It was considered the most basic tenet of our bicameral system of government—two separate houses of power beholden to two uniquely different constituencies. Senators were elected by the state legislatures to protect states' rights and keep a check on the balance of power over the federal government. This issue was at the very heart of the debate over the new American system of government. During the Constitutional Convention, powerful arguments stated that all purely democratic forms of government, wherein every leader was chosen by a majority of voters, would fundamentally overwhelm, weaken, and eventually destroy the system. This had been observed in democracy after democracy throughout history.

The original clause in Section 3 of the Constitution states as follows:

> *The Senate of the United States shall be composed of two Senators from each State, chosen by the Legislature thereof, for six Years; and each Senator shall have one Vote.*

During the Constitutional Convention of 1787, a number of proposals were considered for how senators should be chosen. Some argued that senatorial selection should be at the discretion of state governors or the House of Representatives or even the President. But the one point that was almost universally agreed upon was that selecting senators should be fundamentally different from the process for choosing congressmen. Only one delegate originally proposed direct senatorial election by popular vote.

Why did the Constitution's authors feel this way? And why so strongly? To better understand why Madison, Jefferson, Washington, Hamilton, Adams, and the others felt so strongly that state legislatures should select their senators, we must first understand why our bicameral form of government—senators and congressmen—was established in the first place. The system was born out of a heated debate between the larger states and the smaller states, with the larger states favoring representation based on population and the smaller states demanding equal representation in government. A brilliant solution was offered that became known as the Connecticut Compromise, or the Great Compromise, wherein representation in the House of Representatives would be based upon the population—more people in the state would mean more people in the House. But the Senate would be based upon the *equal* representation of each state. All states would have the same number of senators. No matter how populous or industrious a state was, they were guaranteed only two senatorial representatives, selected by their state legislatures.

Because congressmen directly represented the people, they would be chosen by popular election. They were not expected to have as much experience or "refinement." They could be younger than senators (25 years vs. 30), and citizens for a shorter period of time (7 years vs. 9). Because senators were chosen by an informed and experienced legislative body, they would serve for a longer term (6 years vs. 2). As explained by James Madison in *The Federalist Papers, Number 62*, senators were to be generally possessed of "a greater extent of information and stability of character." This was viewed as the best way to balance power among the people, the states, and the federal government. Because the states held authority over the composition of the Senate, it was seen as a means whereby the states could check federal power.

Convention delegate George Mason of Virginia, considered along with James Madison as the "Father of the Bill of Rights" argued that "allowing [the states] to appoint the second branch of the National Legislature [the Senate]" would offer the states "some means of defending themselves against encroachments of the National Government".1 Thus, by making senators accountable to their respective legislatures it tended to make them more hesitant to support any federal legislation that might prove invasive of the rights and prerogatives of their state's authority. James Madison is quoted as saying, "The Senate will be elected absolutely and exclusively by the State Legislatures." and will therefore "owe its existence more or less to the favor of the State Governments, and must consequently feel a dependence" on them in order to retain their seats in the future.2

There was no question where each senator's allegiance should have been. When ratification of the Constitution was held in New York, Alexander Hamilton explained that "Senators will constantly look up to the state governments with an eye of dependence and affection. If they are ambitious to continue in office, they will make every prudent arrangement for this purpose, and, whatever may be their private sentiments or politics, they will be convinced that the surest means of obtaining reelection will be a uniform attachment to the interests of their several states." He stated succinctly that a senator's "future is absolutely in the power of the states," and asked, "Will not this form a powerful check?3 The plan was ingenious, and in my view *inspired*.

So what happened? Why was this logic entirely annulled in 1913?

THE ERA OF BIG GOVERNMENT BEGINS

The 17th Amendment now reads:

> *The Senate of the United States shall be composed of two Senators from each State, elected by the people thereof, for six years; and each Senator shall have one vote.*

Prior to 1913 the process of senatorial selection gave to states the power to promote or halt the process of ratifying amendments. This power was held indirectly through the U.S. Senate and directly through state legislatures.

Also prior to 1913 the President had to acquire the Senate's "advice and consent" when appointing Supreme Court judges, which meant that states held powerful sway in a branch of government wherein they could never be directly represented. Prior to 1913, the states directly influenced the ratification of any treaty because such ratifications required a two-thirds senatorial majority. For example, when the inequitable terms of peace were established and supported by President Woodrow Wilson at the Treaty of Versailles after World War I, the states had no say, despite the objection of many state and local politicians back home.

Prior to 1913 the states could influence Congress's ability to raise and support a military, regulate piracy, and intercede in "offences against the law of nations." They had direct regulative authority in international commerce, the declaration of war, and matters of foreign policy that affected their states.

Before 1913, states wielded vast influence through their senatorial representatives to shape and effectively veto any unwise federal action. However, after 1913, such powers were effectively abdicated, and senators by definition became no different from their congressional counterparts. The state legislatures lost their power to restrain the federal government, to influence legislation, and to act as the safeguard they were meant to be. Actually, the Senate is now free of almost any accountability except to those who give them financial support. They are becoming more and more aligned with the executive branch to promote the exercise of power beyond the President's constitutional constraints.

It had long been understood that a bicameral legislature was less likely to concoct foolish or unjust legislation. This was because both bodies had to agree upon any law before it could pass. Some might wonder, "Wouldn't this make it practically impossible to pass anything whatsoever?" But this was exactly the point! Our Founders felt this should be precisely what should take place. New laws should be *difficult* to pass. The process demanded a much more sober and careful consideration of every lawmaking procedure.

Bicameralism also yielded additional benefits that stopped oppressive laws dead in their tracks. As explained in the *Federalist Papers, Number 51*, the idea was "to divide the legislature into different branches; and to render them by different modes of election, and different principles of action, as little connected with each other, as the nature of their common functions and their common dependencies on the society, will admit."

Few Americans now contemplate a time when the U.S. Senate was accountable to State Legislatures. Yet when this situation existed it greatly reduced the ability of special interests to influence government for their own private gains. Because they were beholden to different constituencies, the House and Senate were remarkably less likely to push through any legislation that benefited a special interest or benefited themselves while harming the public good. It may have been possible to gain support for a bad resolution from one legislative body through manipulation, deception, or bribery, but it would be much more difficult to gain the support of both.

Madison further expressed his faith in this mechanism by stating:

> *"[T]he improbability of sinister combinations will be in proportion to the dissimilarity in the genius of the two bodies, it must be politic to distinguish them from each other by every circumstance which will consist with a due harmony in all proper measures and with the genuine principle of republican government."*

How then was it possible that the 17th Amendment came about? How did our lawmakers of the early part of the twentieth century entirely forget or ignore such foundational pillars that supported the bicameral legislative branches of our republic form of government?

As I said before, we must consider the times in which the amendment was passed. The ideologies of populist democracy, progressivism, and socialism were sweeping through the government and general citizenry in a way that had never been imagined. If any single politician can be directly associated with the 17th Amendment's passage, that man would be William Jennings Bryan. However, he cannot be considered the only villain. A natural and effective orator, his motives were genuinely sincere at the time he expressed them, though his integrity was often questioned by his adversaries.

Bryan ran for, and was defeated, in his efforts to win the Presidency as a Democrat on three occasions (1896, 1900, and 1908). He served two terms in the United States House of Representatives from Nebraska and even as Secretary of State in the first term of Woodrow Wilson. However, he resigned in protest after the United States entered World War I. He was a progressive Democrat and became known as the "great commoner" because of his overwhelming faith in the wisdom of the common people. This, of course, was a direct contradiction of the wisdom of our Founders who felt that the majority could indeed be wrongly influenced by whims, emotions, and sentiments, often favoring the majority while trampling upon the minority.

The Founding Fathers believed that even governments that claimed accountability to the people were no less prone to corruption than are monarchies or aristocracies. Madison was quite clear in his stance that governments should never be placed entirely in the people's hands:

> *"A common passion or interest will, in almost every case, be felt by a majority of the whole; a communication and concert results from the form of government itself; and there is nothing to check the inducements to sacrifice the weaker part or an obnoxious individual. Hence it is that such democracies have ever been spectacles of turbulence and contention; have ever (been) found incompatible with personal security or the rights of property; and have in general been as short in their lives as they have been violent in their deaths."*

William Jennings Bryan may have also had personal reasons for advocating the 17th Amendment. In his bid to become Nebraska's Senator in 1894, he was soundly rejected by Nebraska's Republican-dominated legislature, despite his undisputed popularity. Still, full blame cannot be laid at his or any other single doorstep.

This was the era often tainted by sensationalized (or "yellow") journalism. Today we may only see such sensationalized periodicals on various newsstands in the checkout lines at our local grocery store. At the turn of the century this kind of journalism dominated virtually every major newspaper, and was probably responsible for instigating the Spanish-American War. When the warship the *USS Maine* sank in Havana's harbor in 1898, American newspapers were quick to tout the headline

"Remember the Maine!" despite the fact that there has never been any evidence that Spain was involved. Yet there were political and economic benefits to the special interests of the day in taking control of Cuba and the Philippines.

The same newspaper magnates who fanned the flames of the Spanish-American War controversy also fanned the flames in their personal crusade to accuse senators of being corrupt to the core. They created in the public mind an image of Senatorial seats being bought and sold by bribery for the benefit of urban political machines. Like the accusations against Spain, these accusations were not well founded. The economic benefits would go to those who changed the constitutional process. It would benefit special interests and bullying politicians at the expense of the various states. These special interests were and are constantly working to manipulate and change the system to work in their favor. Unfortunately, it is human nature to manipulate one's point of view, which was one of the tendencies that the Founding Fathers fought so hard to prevent.

Of the 1,180 senators elected between 1787 and 1909, only fifteen of these seats were contested due to allegations of corruption or bribery, and only seven cases resulted in a senator being denied his seat—a rather impressive record considering that the House of Representatives, even though its members were chosen by popular election, had a total of 382 seats contested for bribery and corruption.

Many also complained that numerous senators were not being seated because of deadlocks in the voting processes of state legislatures. The Constitution only states that a Senator should be chosen by the State Legislature. It did not specify the method for how this should be conducted. States with a bicameral legislature voted for senators during a joint meeting, while those with one house voted as a single body. Still others required a concurring vote in both of its houses. Problems sometimes arose when the two houses were controlled by different parties and could not reach a compromise. This problem was terribly aggravated by a federal law passed in 1866, just after the end of the Civil War. The federal government had gained strength, and it required by law that the bicameral state legislatures meet separately and take a voice vote. If either house was not in agreement they were required to meet jointly the next day, and every day after that, until the matter was settled. This law also required that a Senatorial candidate win an absolute majority, which could be difficult if more than two candidates sought the office. By requiring the first vote to be publicly voiced, the 1866 law revealed who each legislator supported, making it easier to organize stonewalling efforts against an undesirable candidate. If legislators proved stubborn in their willingness to compromise, securing a majority became impossible. Between 1885 and 1912, there were seventy-one instances where a state legislature was deadlocked. Seventeen Senate seats went unfilled for one legislative session or more.

Such deadlocks were hyped by the media and convinced many Americans that senators ought to be elected directly by the people. Deadlocks of this nature might have been easily avoided by altering the 1866 law to allow a plurality of votes or for a second vote for the top two candidates to win a Senatorial seat. Unfortunately, this didn't seem to occur to many of the people in power at that time. State legislatures became convinced that the only way to end deadlocks and guarantee their state's representation was to yield to the concept of popular elections, thereby forfeiting, theoretically for all time, their only means of forestalling the inevitable expansion of federal powers.

During these decades, socialists attacked the government on every front, believing that its leadership was fundamentally corrupt, controlled by the rich, and hopelessly out of touch with average Americans. Socialists believed that any problems facing the government could be solved by making its institutions more democratic. This was a great departure from the beliefs of the framers of the Constitution, who felt that concentrating too much power in the hands of any single entity, including a popular majority, would result in abuse and tyranny. The Founding Fathers took deliberate steps to dilute the power of the majority, and insulate at least one body of the legislature—the Senate—from the capricious passions of the people.

Thinking himself wiser than the Founding Fathers, William Jennings Bryan argued that "If the people of the United States have enough intelligence to choose their representatives in the State legislatures . . . they have enough intelligence to choose the men who shall represent them in the United States Senate."

This campaign by Bryan and others for direct election of senators finally succeeded. It was decided at both the federal and state levels that a Constitutional amendment was needed to fix these perceived problems.

In one of the great ironies of history, the legislatures of the various states proved to be not only willing, but enthusiastic accomplices to their own disenfranchisement. Until 1913, the ability to select its own senators had been the primary means by which states could check the power of the federal government. Yet the states blindly ratified the 17th Amendment, thus aiding "in their own collective suicide," as they "slashed their own throats and destroyed federalism forever."

In another sad irony, the final or 36th state to ratify the amendment was Connecticut, the very state that in 1887 had inspired the Great Compromise that insured that the House and Senate would be loyal to separate constituencies. Two states that voted to strike down the amendment were Utah and Delaware. States that refused to take up the issue included Florida, Kentucky, Mississippi, Rhode Island, Georgia, Virginia, and South Carolina.

With the Senate's structure fundamentally altered, it could no longer fulfill its functions as intended. The states, now lacking any real voice beyond that of any other special interest, had lost the power to protect themselves and the Union. It wasn't long before all the states were at the mercy of the federal government, whose policies became more and more intrusive. As special interests flourished, they found it increasingly easy to ransack the national Treasury. With power now concentrated in the hands of fewer people, opportunistic majorities have managed to promote their own interests at the expense of minorities and individuals. The federal government can now be seen in nearly every segment of American life: commerce, education, health care, transportation, communication, police protection—all areas that were once principally the domain of state governments.

The continual use of unfunded mandates by the federal government places an enormous burden upon state governments, often forcing them to pay for programs they don't need or want, a practice that a pre-17th Amendment Senate would have assuredly restrained.

The era of big government is often presumed to have begun with Franklin D. Roosevelt's New Deal. In reality, government's steady and persistent growth began right after World War I. Federal growth rates had always spiked during times of war, but during those times of peace between 1787 and 1913, government growth was virtually non-existent. Within a single decade after the passage of the 17ᵗʰ Amendment, the government experienced consistent growth even when there was no national crisis.

Certainly the Great Depression and the New Deal spiked a growth rate in the size of the federal government. Unfortunately, we have never turned back, and government growth continues to accelerate. Everyone now looks to the federal government to fix everything. Government bureaucracy is now an American way of life, and its expansive beginnings coincide remarkably with the ratification of the 17ᵗʰ Amendment. Furthermore, senators must now conduct expensive state-wide campaigns to reach the voters, forcing them to become far more willing to make deals with special interests and political machines who will fund and organize their campaigns. As stated above, another phenomenon is that the U.S. Senate majority has gone into league with the President of their own party, creating another unchecked and overbalanced concentration of power.

Unprecedented growth has meant that temporary majorities have managed to force Congress to pass unhealthy and often illegitimate legislation, even if it endangered the economic or political rights of individuals, businesses, or smaller factions. It seems no coincidence that both the 16ᵗʰ and 17ᵗʰ Amendments were ratified the same year as the Federal Reserve Act and the League of Nations.

Attempts to reduce the size of government through legislation will never be more than Band-Aids while these amendments remain in place. The federal government's predisposition to expand will continue unabated until the original vision of our Founding Fathers and the Constitution's structural safeguards are reestablished and cemented back in place.

THE SILENT ARTILLERY OF TIME

As stated before, the year 1913 saw a perfect storm of socialism and populism mingled with American nationalism and secularism, alongside trendy new style of politics called progressivism. As a result, many American politicians drew a philosophical blank—entirely forgetting the logic and rationale upon which our nation was founded. Keep in mind that these same social and political movements were also trending in Europe. In many ways, they can be tied directly to the misunderstandings and arrogance that led to World War I—a conflict which later took the world into World War II.

In some ways I believe these wars actually aided in the survival of the American experiment, but not for the reasons many might suppose. I believe these conflicts stemmed the tide of socialism and secularism in the United States only for another generation or two. Communism and the Cold War also served to keep this sickness at bay before these infections could fully overwhelm the nation. However, with the fall of the Soviet Union, the flaws adopted into the system over the last 100 years have been allowed to flourish like never before. The disaster of 9/11 helped a little by rekindling the American spirit of patriotism, pride and unity. However, in some ways we may have become too proud and somewhat boastful. It's been surprising for me to witness how quickly our spirit of unity from 9/11 faded. Every day, it seems we find ourselves enveloped in a state of dysfunction that threatens the foundation of the country. But, I believe that it's not too late.

One of my highest priorities as President would be to repeal these misguided Amendments, but in a manner that creates as little pain as possible, primarily by placing the authorities and responsibilities usurped by the federal government back into the hands of the states as the Constitution originally intended.

Can it be done? Yes it can! Moreover, I believe it will be an incredible shock to many Americans as they see how many of our growing and repeatedly revolving problems suddenly and miraculously diminish and resolve themselves.

In 1838, Abraham Lincoln gave a speech in which he lamented the fading comprehension of the republican principles upon which our nation was founded. He observed that the country's institutions and structures were increasingly being misinterpreted and misunderstood. He believed the structures upon which our nation had been built "were a fortress of strength; but what invading foemen could never do, the silent artillery of time has done; the leveling of its walls."

To me this accurately and poignantly describes what is again presently happening in America. This time we are losing a great war against oppressive government from within. Only through education and enlightenment can these problems be rooted out and rectified. To do this, it will require the leadership of a president who recognizes the disease and its causes—one who has the courage to prescribe and implement an effective cure.

Until these two cancerous tumors are removed, we won't really be able to start to heal as a nation. We will only become more and more polarized and socialistic. We will never be able to solve our debt and other economic problems. We won't be able to shrink the federal government to its proper size and effectively work on solving our social problems. We are definitely on the wrong path and we need to repeal these two amendments to start to get back on the right path— the patriot's path.

I have confidence that the American people can recognize the need to repeal the 16th and 17th Amendments to the U.S. Constitution. We must solve the problems of taxation without limitation and to restore to the states' their balance of power. To do this, we must unite and focus on the roots of these problems and not just constantly debate superficially, never really making a difference or solving anything. We have much work to do. So, let's get it done, NOW!

Chapter 13

Bullying and More Bullying

A SECONDARY STATUS

I've saved this material until last because, in an important way, I've already presented my most important arguments for becoming President. I've already offered the most common sense solutions to solving America's problems. I'm very much focused on the large issues, and I sincerely believe that if we resolve the biggest problems facing America, many of the issues and challenges mentioned in this chapter will resolve themselves.

Nevertheless, I hope my positions on various issues will help you to understand me better as a person. I believe one of the most important principles that has been handily swept aside by modern politicians is the idea that the person's private life can be separated from that person's public life. In other words, popular opinion seems to suggest that the choices that someone makes in his or her private life have no effect upon decisions or abilities as a politician or leader.

No one is perfect, and I am the first to admit that I am not perfect. I have faults and struggles that I seek to overcome every day. Having said that, I'm not suggesting that I have fatal or glaring flaws. Undoubtedly, some will look for skeletons in my closet, but as I stated earlier, as a Patriot, as a Christian—and as a human being—I am striving to walk the walk as well as talk the talk. I am not concerned about the efforts of journalists and others to find evidence of wrongdoing, immorality, or illegal activities in my past. If a candidate is guilty of some gross offense—either legally or morally—in most cases this might disqualify that person from office. However, I cannot judge, but strive to forgive all people of their trespasses and ask forgiveness for mine. Having said that, I believe as a voter, it's perfectly acceptable to expect be able to vote for a man or woman who is not only an upright human being and a staunch defender of the Constitution, but who has also lived in an exemplary way and treated others properly—in public and in private.

America on the whole is a very forgiving nation. If a leader stands forth and admits to wrongdoing, most citizens are generally willing to overlook it, but there are some powerful reasons to make "character" one of the more important attributes that we look for in a leader. Some might mock this, but "what goes around comes around." I believe that good thoughts and behavior translate into good decisions. If a person's life is fogged by crimes or immorality, their "clarity" will be affected when it comes to making critical decisions. Some may balk at such a philosophy, believing it has no basis. However, in my life I've too often witnessed the effects of unacknowledged wrongdoing. Leaving such matters unresolved will have a corrosive and cancerous effect upon people, their leadership, and eventually the whole nation. I hope to renew and refresh your conviction that *character matters*. I personally believe that it matters more than anything else—even more than issues, personal charisma, oratorical skills or any other leadership quality.

I'd like now to mention a few issues that relate to character.

BULLIES AND COWARDS

When I was a young man I vividly remember being consumed by feelings of anger and resentment toward others. Much of this was caused by bullying that happened to me because my father was a teacher at our high school in Blackfoot, Idaho.

I was just a little boy when a few of the high school students who didn't like my father decided to take their anger out on me. As a teacher my dad always insisted upon courtesy, discipline, and obedience. He was bald, so they called him "Chromedome." I remember occasionally being taunted, slapped, and pushed around by these high school students. They would try to humiliate and hurt me, all because they must have been frustrated that they were not doing better in my father's classes. As a young boy, I never understood why they were picking on me and never told anyone about this abuse. I was afraid, and sometimes embarrassed, that my father was just a poor teacher instead of a wealthy and respected doctor or lawyer like the parents of some of my friends.

My father was always willing to tear tickets at the high school games and took me along because he knew I loved sports. He always remained behind to close things up, and I went on ahead and walked home. On one snowy winter night after a high school basketball game, I was walking home alone, headed north up the east side of Fisher Street. It was a beautiful night and lights glowed from these beautiful homes. My mood was up and my spirits high because our team had just won the game. I remember the very spot where a car pulled over and several young men jumped out, tackled me to the ground, and washed my face in snow. I did my best to protect myself as they slapped me while shouting curses and accusations against "Chromedome." I was stunned and physically hurt, but their words ringing in my ears also hurt. This gang of young men vanished as quickly as they arrived, leaving me lying in the snow. I cried all the way home and went straight to bed without talking to anyone.

Because of this and other events I began to internalize general feelings of anger, distrust, and resentment. These emotions seemed to dominate my attitude for several years. The turning point for me, as I've previously stated, was seeing the movies *Mary Poppins* and *The Sound of Music*. These movies and their songs spoke to my soul and helped transform my attitude into one of wanting to make the world a better place and not allow my anger to drag me down.

I've experienced bullies all of my life in many different environments—education, employment, religion and politics. These experiences have made me particularly sensitive to the struggles of those who are oppressed for no other reason than because the oppressor is stronger.

SAME-SEX MARRIAGE

The current issue of same sex marriage captures the attention of the media. Many citizens hold firm convictions that this civil rights issue should be supported and promoted. In the end, I believe this is a moral issue which should be decided by the individual states and localities. I personally believe that *marriage* should be protected by its Divine or traditional definitions, and that *other rights* such as housing, employment, etc., should be matters of equal opportunity. No one should be discriminated against for their feelings and inclinations. All parties have protected rights to express and advocate their convictions.

It's not an issue that should be dictated by the federal government.

To deny that certain parts of the country have values that do not support same-sex marriage is to deny present-day reality. I intend to steer clear of issues that will resolve themselves if we returned to the principles of the Constitution and repealed amendments that impede the Constitution's intended checks and balances. The reason I'm particularly concerned with this issue is because it relates closely to the issue I just discussed—bullies and cowards—and the desire of the strong to take advantage of the weak. Bulling is not appropriate, regardless of who is doing it.

In that regard I believe there should be zero tolerance that anyone should live in fear of bullies because of their race, gender, religion or sexual orientation. This is a country based first and foremost upon equality, tolerance and love for our fellow citizens. However, creating laws to protect specific groups does not strengthen an individual's existing constitutional rights.

The federal government has no business defining marriage or family. Likewise, we cannot allow those who favor the traditional family to be ostracized and punished because they profess those beliefs or conduct their lives and operate their businesses based on such beliefs. There seems to be a new tendency in America to define a bully as someone who merely expresses an opinion or conducts their life based upon a certain value system. Having personally experienced the fear, anger, isolation and the loneliness of being the victim of bullies, I know that those who express support of traditional values are not the kinds of bullies I experienced. A bully is someone who inflicts pain, humiliation, abuse, and ridicule.

The very fabric of America is based upon rejecting this kind of prejudice and enforcing laws against it. What I fear is that the political pendulum may now be swinging too far the other way, and those who have been oppressed are seeking to become the oppressors. We cannot tolerate the latter any more than we can tolerate the former. Americans must become more vigilant as a people to make certain that basic rights of life, liberty, and the pursuit of happiness are protected—no matter someone's race, religion, gender, sexual orientation, or personal opinions.

THE DEBT CEILING

Right now the national debt of the United States is higher than it has ever been. Congress continues to debate the issue of the debt ceiling, or how much debt the United States should be allowed to have. There should be *no* debt ceiling. Why? Because there should be *no debt.* If we are the greatest nation on earth, why are we in so much debt? Why are we borrowing from wealthy nations to give to poor nations?

Billionaire Warren Buffett supposedly offered one of the best statements about the debt ceiling I have heard. He said, "I could end the deficit in five minutes. You just pass a law that says that anytime there is a deficit of more than 3% of GDP, all sitting members of Congress are ineligible for re-election."

I agree and propose that the President should also be included in this. Not only will this eliminate debt, it will stimulate the economy and make all politicians think carefully before voting on going to war (a measure that requires sudden and massive investments).

The 26th Amendment (granting 18-year-olds the right to vote) took only three months and eight days to be ratified. Why? It was simple – because the people demanded it. That was in 1971, before computers, e-mail, cell phones, etc. Of the twenty-seven amendments to the Constitution, seven of them took one year or less to become the law of the land, all because of public pressure. Today, a law eliminating national debt could be passed in the same period of time. This checks the power of congress and gives power back to the people.

FEDERAL RESERVE

As they become aware, Americans are appalled to learn that Congress delegated to the Federal Reserve all of its Section 8 rights to "coin money*" and "regulate the value thereof"* as outlined in the Constitution. Like any other federal department or agency, the Federal Reserve needs open and comprehensive audits and restrictions on printing and pumping money into the economy, manipulating interest rates, making questionable deals with foreign and domestic banks, and interfering with the free market system. Congress must take back these rights and shoulder its responsibilities to manage the Federal Reserve or end it altogether.

There is no greater threat to the security and prosperity of the United States today than the out-of-control and secretive Federal Reserve banking system. The government has entrusted the nation's financial future to this institution. It was established as America's central bank by the Federal Reserve Act snuck through Congress on Christmas Eve, 1913—the very same year that the 16th and 17th Amendments to the Constitution were added. This was no coincidence. Repealing both of these amendments would help to diminish the Federal Reserve's power.

What you could buy with $1.00 in 1913 now costs $22.55. The Fed manipulates interest rates, interferes with the free market, and fuels our boom-and-bust economy. It helped bring about the housing bubble and financial collapse of 2007-2008 by keeping funds flowing to reckless bureaucracies like Fannie Mae and Freddie Mac. It enables banks to hook individuals and businesses with loans on projects not in demand or not viable. With each economic challenge, the FED has not changed its policies. They simply direct the U.S. Treasury to print more money and tell the citizens that a recovery will never be realized unless the federal government is willing to orchestrate huge bailouts.

Monetary policy reform must include televised open-market committee meetings of the Federal Reserve. All Board of Governors of the Federal Reserve should continue to make weekly information reports of M3 monetary aggregate and its components, including large deposits. The money supply is measured by standardized monetary aggregates. These are: M0 = cash and coin; M1 = M0 + demand deposits; M2 = M1 + savings deposits and money market shares; and M3 = larger (> \$100,000) time deposits and institutional funds, which have not been tracked since 2006. It must also require us to return to sound money as a competing currency based on a Composite Commodity.

Congress presently lacks any authority to audit or control the FED—a direct contradiction of the intentions of our Founding Fathers. The Feds are accountable to no individual, no entity, and no legislative body. It's time for a comprehensive audit that will correctly change or end this system and process. This will enable America to move toward economic security, financial responsibility, and lasting prosperity.

HEALTH CARE

This is an *issue-de-jour* that I have a keen and particular interest in resolving. I believe most Americans feel the same. There's no question that the healthcare industry needs to be improved.

But Americans deserve a government that does not devalue or weaken the present system. Patients should receive the best care available. The doctor-patient relationship is vital and must be protected. For the last generation, the burning question has been how this should be accomplished. Unfortunately, we are faced with a health care program that was rammed through as a solution, but is ultimately destructive to the system and is unsustainable. Everyone must accept blame. The opposition parties, when in power, did not resolve this problem when they had the power and the opportunity. They allowed problems to further escalate. So in some ways, we got what we got because those with better ideas did not act.

We must redraft the Affordable Care Act into a document that can be read and understood by all. As James Madison stated, "It will be of little avail to the people . . . if laws be so voluminous that they cannot be read, or so incoherent that they cannot be understood." Therefore, with regard to the Affordable Care Act, we must keep the best and discard the rest. No one wins where there is excessive government control and forced mandates.

The federal government should not be allowed to track Americans' medical records from cradle to grave The Food and Drug Administration (FDA) and the Federal Trade Commission (FTC) should not be interfering with Americans' knowledge of and access to alternative treatments and to dietary supplements. The collusion of these organizations and large pharmaceutical companies are keeping many valuable and needed treatments and cures from the market. Such intrusions force doctors to move from a patient-care model to a business-care model. Insurance becomes more expensive to purchase and more difficult to maintain. As politicians trade influence for favors, patients are left with less protection and with more frustration. Industry oversight, reasonable limits on litigated damages, and doctor-patient shared malpractice insurance must be part of the final formula.

The answer to our nation's health crisis lies in freedom— not force. Insurance should be available for purchase across state lines. All Americans should be eligible for Health Savings Accounts (HSAs) and remove government-imposed barriers for the same. Everyone could pay a reasonable amount into an insurance fund used for catastrophic emergencies and terminal illness. The patient, family, doctor, and insurance company could all participate in treatment decisions. Finally, monies paid for Medicare and Medicaid should be safeguarded and not be used for any other purpose.

1. A sustainable health care solution must include the following:
2. Prohibit insurance companies from imposing lifetime benefit limits on a customer.
3. Give individuals the freedom of purchasing the health care plan that best suits their needs.
4. Return the power of regulating health insurance to the states.
5. The ratio of premium payments by older or unhealthy individuals to younger and healthier individuals should be returned to at least five to one instead of three to one.
6. Offer dependent coverage up to age 25.
7. Prevent customers with a pre-existing condition from being denied coverage if they can show proof of continuous coverage, including COBRA.
8. Provide a one-time open enrollment period each year.
9. Increase purchasing power for small businesses and individuals by providing a targeted tax credit which can be solely used for the purchase of health insurance.
10. Require transparency from the medical and insurance companies regarding the costs of procedures.

The most important thing to understand is that it's not too late to fix what is broken by sustaining the constitution. However, if it's not fixed now, it may soon be too late. Together we can resolve this problem for the betterment of our own lives and future generations.

ILLEGAL IMMIGRATION

I am enthusiastically in favor of and will support *legal* immigration. Immigrants are the life-blood of America. The American dream is not a pie of limited size that must be hoarded in order to be preserved. We should invite those who love liberty, religious freedom, and who want to work and prosper to come and join with us as citizens.

But let them come for *these reasons* and with a determination to become Americans. Let them come to pledge allegiance to the Constitution of the United States of America, to the flag, and to the republic for which it stands. Let them come to learn English and to be loyal to no other country.

Every country has immigration laws that should be respected and enforced. The United States has created several immigration problems that need to be addressed for workers who were encouraged to come the U.S. to work, but not given permanent status:

- Keeping families of workers together.
- Strict documentation process or immigration law enforcement for those who came or stayed illegally.
- Automatic citizenship for children born to illegal immigrants in the United States.
- Federal, state and local permissive approach to addressing illegal immigration issues.

We need to promote legal immigration and end illegal immigration in order to:

- Protect our citizens, economy and culture.
- Prevent our country, states and communities from being forced to absorb illegal aliens.
- Stop the financial drain and negative impact on our economy.
- Begin receiving economic vitality and revenues from happy and productive workers.

We can do this by doing the following:

- Respect states' rights and American citizens' civil liberties.
- Promote legal immigration and punish illegal immigration.
- Secure all borders and points of entry and deport all who have criminal records.
- Establish English as the national language and insure cultural integration and loyalty to the U.S.
- Document every prospective immigrant for travel, work or immigration/citizenship status.
- Discourage illegal alien women from coming to the U.S. in order to give birth to children on U.S. soil so the children will automatically be U.S. citizens. This can be done through simple testing prior to entry and carefully monitoring those who visit.
- Grant legal work status to every person arriving and living in the U.S. prior to December 31, 2014.
- Grant three (3) years (until 12/31/17) to apply for citizenship, behind those already legally in line.
- If those granted three (3) years have not applied and qualified for citizenship by 12/31/17, they will be deemed illegal aliens.

- Those arriving on or after January 1, 2015 will be considered illegal aliens.

In 1907 Theodore Roosevelt said:

"We should insist that if the immigrant who comes here in good faith becomes an American and assimilates himself to us, he shall be treated on an exact equality with everyone else, for it is an outrage to discriminate against any such man because of creed, or birthplace, or origin. But this is predicated upon the person's becoming in every facet an American and nothing but an American . . . There can be no divided allegiance here. Any man who says he is an American, but something else also, isn't an American at all. We have room for but one flag, the American flag . . . We have room for but one language here, and that is the English language . . . and we have room for but one sole loyalty, and that is a loyalty to the American people."

We must immediately adopt an effective plan to reduce and stop illegal immigration. We must have a reasonable time and opportunity to assimilate citizens into our economy, society, and culture. Allowing illegal immigration will not solve world poverty, nor will it enrich our nation. We can best help other countries by being a good example, teaching constitutional principles and self-reliance, and serving them by means of our individual free will and not by federal foreign aid.

Also, we must be willing to follow through and restrict those who come here illegally, commit crimes, or refuse to pledge their complete loyalty to the U.S. Constitution. If such are discovered, we must reject them, deport them, or punish them according to their crimes. Repeat offenders should spend jail time in a sub-contracted neutral foreign prison. This would be far cheaper, more efficient, and more effective.

LEGITIMATE LEGISLATION

Let no bills be signed into law that cannot be read and understood by any reasonable person. I see no reason why any bill should be longer than the U.S. Constitution itself. Each legislator should read and understand a bill before debating it and voting on it. This can easily be enforced through good faith, along with a brief test that each legislator should perform prior to presenting a bill before the floor for debate and vote. Such examination should be part of the public Congressional Record. This will go far to eliminate the pork-barrel programs that are often inserted into the original legislation that might otherwise be useful and productive.

I make every American this promise: As President, I will veto any law that is not reasonable in size and able to be understood by "the reasonable man." It is vital to our republic that citizens can read and comprehend the law, debate it, and live it. Laws that are too long, too complicated, and open to a multitude of interpretations are not good. I will veto any law that is not "certified simple." They must pass the test of length, clarity, and purpose. If they do not pass the Certified Simple Test, they will be vetoed.

We are free to choose to create and obey constitutional law and live in freedom. If we create unconstitutional or illegitimate laws, we forfeit some of our freedom and must live with the consequences. Some illegitimate laws may have parts that are good, but if it is not constitutional in its entirety, it should and must be rejected in its entirety. We have a tremendous responsibility to be vigilant and to protect our freedoms and the Constitution.

In their wisdom, our Founding Fathers provided a check and balance system so that ill-conceived and illegitimate laws could be negated. If, in their opinions, the justices of the Supreme Court find parts of a law that are legitimate and constitutional, they can comment and thus guide the legislative and the executive branches in the future. However, if a law is not constitutional in its entirety, it must be struck down in its entirety so Congress can begin again. Otherwise the Supreme Court has the power to create laws *a la carte*. This was never the purpose nor the authority of our highest court.

For example, the Affordable Care Act (ACA) was illegitimate and unconstitutional from its inception. Why? Simple. Because no one had read it! The majority leader in the U.S. Senate said that we needed to pass this law and *then* find out what was in it. Neither the sponsors nor the opponents of the law had read it. The Republicans opposed it primarily because the Democrats had proposed it. Maybe some of their staff members had read portions of it, but few or none had read all 2,000+ pages or really understood all of its minutiae or how it would affect the whole. No Senator or Representative read or understood the bill in its entirety before the law was brought to a vote. Amendments that had nothing to do with the bill were quickly added just before passage.

The bill is illegitimate, and parts are blatantly unconstitutional. The President eagerly wanted it passed and signed it into law. Even the *President* hadn't read it. When does a President or legislator have time to read a 2000+ page book? If any one of them had been given an exam on what the bill contained, they would all have failed the test.

We should immediately reject any bill that any citizen, parent, teacher or student cannot read, understand and discuss. This is the test of understanding. I will veto any bill that has not been read by members of the House and the Senate who vote on it. I will demand that their vote signifies the same. The public must hold their public servants accountable to do their homework and be honest in how they do it. If they don't do their homework, they should flunk, be suspended or expelled. If we don't demand this, we deserve what we get. Heaven help us if there is ever another Constitutional Convention. We would assuredly end up with a 10 volume constitution that no one would ever read or understand.

Chapter 14

America's Future

NATIVE AMERICANS

I want to be the President of our Native American citizens if they will have me. They have suffered and endured much. Each individual, each tribe, and each nation needs to step up to embrace the greatness that belongs to them. Their vision has been blurred by many lies and broken promises. Their path to peace and happiness has been clouded by a history of defeat and heartbreak. Their trail has been washed away by tears and substance abuse. Their desire to progress has been suppressed by the boundaries of the reservation. Something must and can be done.

As a young boy, I grew up next to the Blackfoot Indian Reservation in southeastern Idaho. I had many Caucasian and Native American friends. As we grew older, I watched happy children, great athletes, and fine students begin to separate themselves and to be separated into different groups. We all took on the traditions, thinking, and behavior of our parents and leaders. We grew apart rather than together. This made me sad and left a yearning inside me to make things right. That yearning remains to this day.

I believe that an important part of our nation's future involves Native Americans. I can't accomplish what needs to be done alone, but I'm confident that we can do it together.

AGRICULTURAL MERRY-GO-ROUND

Agriculture is fundamental to the American way of life. It's particularly close to my heart because of my Idaho boyhood in "the Potato Capital of the World." Since it is rarely discussed by politicians seeking the highest office in the land, I feel it is appropriate to discuss it here.

America's farming industry is large enough and strong enough and has ample information to allow producers to regulate themselves as an industry. The federal government should not be in control of our food supply, nor mandate what we eat. Farmers don't want subsidies; they want fair market value for their products at the marketplace. Government should never pay farmers *not* to produce, a policy that began in the early part of the twentieth century as socialism was creeping into many societies across the globe. The American agriculture industry should not be a political or partisan issue. It should be an individual producer and consumer issue operating in a free market. It should not be for sale to benefit special interests over individual or national interests.

Social welfare programs should not be part of the political agriculture landscape. The farm bill Congress just passed this year (2014) is a monument to Washington's dysfunction and an insult to taxpayers, consumers, and citizens. Defenders of this bill say it was a compromise. But this is only half true. This thousand-page, trillion-dollar mess is less a compromise between House Republicans and Senate Democrats than it is collusion between both parties against the American people. The motivation was to benefit the special interests at the expense of our national interest and the personal interests of our citizens.

This was the year the farm bill was supposed to be different. This was supposed to be the year when we would finally split the bill into its logical component pieces and reform them one at a time. This was the year we might have strengthened the original food stamps welfare program with work requirements. This was the year we might have made sure wealthy Americans were no longer eligible for food stamps. Such reforms aren't in the bill that was passed. Many of the few improvements the House and Senate initially tried to include were removed during the secretive conference committee process. It was a lost opportunity all around. The farm bill continues to be a troubling trend in Washington: using raw political power to twist public policy against the American people to profit political and corporate insiders.

For example, under this legislation the federal government will continue to force taxpayers to subsidize sugar companies, both through the tax code and at the grocery store. This bill creates an artificial crisis each time Congress considers a farm bill—a crisis used to avoid genuine oversight and extract campaign contributions for incumbent politicians. Under this farm bill, small, independent Christmas tree farmers will now be required to pay a special tax to a government-created organization controlled by larger, corporate producers. These costs will, of course, be passed on to working families. The agriculture bill thus includes a modern public version of *A Christmas Carol* by Charles Dickens. So now, every December, Washington will, in effect, rob the Cratchit family to pay Mr. Scrooge and his lobbyists.

I must also mention the farm bill's most offensive feature: its bullying, disenfranchising shakedown of the American West. Here's how it works. More than 50 percent of all the land west of the Mississippi River is controlled by federal bureaucracy and cannot be developed. No homes. No businesses. No communities or community centers. No farms or farmers' markets. No hospitals or colleges or schools. No little league fields or playgrounds. Nothing! In many western states a huge portion, seventy to ninety percent (70-90%) of their land isn't theirs. To compensate local governments for the tax revenue that Washington unfairly denies them, Congress created the PILT program, which stands for Payment In Lieu of Taxes. Under PILT, Congress sends a few cents on the dollar out West every year to make up for lost property taxes these communities might otherwise collect.

Local governments across the western United States completely depend upon Congress making good on this promise. This year, knowing the importance of such funding for western states, Congress inserted PILT into the bill in order to extort political concessions from their congressmen and senators, like some two-bit protection racket. "Shucks, that's a nice fire department you got there," government bureaucracies say to western communities. "Nice school your kids have. Be a shame if you didn't qualify for the funds you need to keep them in operation." Communities, counties and states are increasingly becoming more and more dependent on the federal government and less and less self-sufficient. The purposes of our Founding Fathers are being frustrated.

This kind of political racketeering in America must come to an end.

ECONOMY AND THE INSOLUBLE BUREAUCRACY

The problem of our bloated bureaucratic network is an issue that will resolve itself if we take the steps I have outlined in former chapters. But because questions about the economy and how to fix it are such an important part of every political campaign, I will take a moment here to outline some basic concepts.

In order to end the economic crisis of inflation, budget deficits, bailouts, and declining dollar value, we need to:

- Repeal the 16th and 17th Amendments
- Balance the budget.
- Eliminate the debt ceiling except in times of war.
- Audit and/or end the Federal Reserve.
- Legalize sound money by returning to a commodity standard including precious metals/minerals, grains, real estate etc.
- Become energy independent.
- Eliminate taxes on income, capital gains, inherited estates.
- Repatriate manufacturing back to the U.S.
- Promote small business development and growth.

The key to America's prosperity is lower taxes, limited government, personal freedom, and sound money. We will all thrive when we all work together to reduce taxes and spending and to reform monetary policy and foreign relations.

Intermediate tax reform should include incentives to invest and grow companies and create jobs. Individuals and companies should be motivated to save money and purchase homes. Death and inheritance taxes and double-taxation should be eliminated.

Spending reform should include freezing non-defense and entitlement spending and reducing overseas military commitments. At the same time, we should strengthen weapons, bases, and troops on our own soil. We must take better care of our veterans.

The federal government needs to get out of the business of controlling business. To bring jobs back to the United States we must allow states to promote innovation, production and small business development. All costly and unnecessary federal regulations should be identified and removed. States and municipalities should monitor and help their own. Individuals and businesses need access to credit and capital through community banks, credit unions, and other financial institutions to foster economic growth, serve their communities and increase individual savings.

Solutions to our nation's economic problems along with the economy in general are notoriously presented to voters as being more complex than they actually are. Many people think their livelihood is dependent upon keeping the illusions of complexity in place. I'm determined to show that the solutions are incredibly simple. We just need to have the willpower to implement them.

EDUCATION

Again, this is a topic getting a lot of attention on social and national media forums. I want to address the matter in a brief way so that everyone knows where I stand.

It is common sense that parents should have the greatest influence over the education of their children. Parents should have the freedom to choose their children's best educational options. No amount of big government spending can or will solve our nation's education problems. One-size-fits-all does not work. It is parents, together with local educators, who must and will solve their problems and provide the best education possible.

Home schooling is a viable and effective alternative to traditional or public education. It can be superior in some ways due to its unique advantages. Families who home school should not be penalized in any manner. Home schooling diplomas should be treated on par with traditional diplomas as long as the students perform well on the entrance exams.

Education has developed into a huge industry focused more on educators and less on students. Many of the causes and activities of educators are unrelated to educating students with a broad education or providing specialized skills. We must stay focused on preparing students for employment and meaningful contributions to society after graduation.

Our federal government has always advanced the idea that every child must have a hot lunch (and now a hot breakfast) and have a guaranteed right to go to college. As a result, student health is suffering and the size of student debt has never been higher. Year after year the idea that every student needs college has markedly depreciated the value of a college diploma. It offers a graduate less hope of preparing for a job that will support a family. Education is best administered by cities and states.

ENERGY AND ENVIRONMENT

There is growing tension between exploration and extracting natural resources and protecting our environment. On the one hand, I promote free market solutions to solving our nation's energy needs instead of allowing government regulations, subsidies, and taxation. However, this only applies to domestic production. I believe heavy tariffs should be imposed on foreign oil imports. The answer to our energy independence is to purchase and/or produce domestic fossil fuel and alternative fuel/energy technologies. We should not restrict domestic production of natural gas, offshore drilling, the use of coal, or even nuclear power. I also believe safety and protection of the environment must receive careful and aggressive attention along with volume of production. After all, our environment today is the only one we will ever have. Energy production and environmental protection are not naturally conflicting forces. They can work hand-in-hand to strengthen our economy and to protect our environment. Consider the following quotes about solar energy:

> *"We're killing people in foreign lands in order to extract 200-million-year- old sunlight (in the form of fossil fuels). We frack our backyards or we blow up our mountaintops . . . for an hour of electricity. When we could just take what's falling free from the sky."*
> - David Kennedy

> *"The use of solar energy has not been opened up because the oil industry does not own the sun."*
> - Ralph Nader

I've heard criticism about wind turbines being eyesores. Some dismiss other forms of alternative energy out of habit. I believe this is a habit born out of a natural prejudice against society's so-called "tree-huggers." Such bias is understandable, but not productive. We should all seek to be responsible stewards of the land, sea and air. We must aggressively protect these natural resources to which we are spiritually and physically bound.

There is no question that pollution and waste is a serious problem, and protecting the environment must be a high priority. Whether or not the environment is threatened by global warming is not the right question. The right question is, "Who can and should control pollution?" Another question is whether or not climate change is man-caused, and if we will sacrifice prosperity to "stop" it. I believe individual citizens, property owners and their respective state governments should control their pollution and manage their natural resources. They should hold polluters accountable in local courts and not face the intimidation, bureaucracy, and expense of fighting the federal government on almost every environmental issue.

FEDERAL LAND

The federal government should turn over its control of massive tracts of land to the respective states. Our government should turn domestic environmental concerns over to the states and focus its efforts on international environmental awareness. We must work closely with other nations to promote the minimization of pollution. We should set the example and help other nations wisely manage global resources. We cannot merely shrug our shoulders in disregard or grind our teeth in resentment because we feel we cannot compete with other countries who seem less concerned with pollution. Nations that neglect the environment will eventually and inevitably pay the high price of that neglect. The United States should lead the way in educating other nations with the philosophy that we all have to live on the same planet and must show that planet equal respect. I'm not naive enough to believe that all nations will do this with willing enthusiasm, but any pressures that the U.S. applies should be based upon wisdom, diplomacy and sound policies. No bullying or contention.

Our primary focus should be directed toward developing renewable energy resources. For more than a century, the United States has stood on the cutting edge of developing these kinds of new technologies based upon free-market ideals, not upon government intervention. No resource, natural or renewable, should receive the support or penalization of the federal government. Such an overseer will ultimately favor certain companies or industries unfairly.

All of us should recognize that once our natural resources are gone, they are *gone*. Our planet's resources must not be wasted.

The first goal of all Americans should be *energy independence.* Energy touches every aspect of our lives. It lubricates the gears of our economy. Our prosperity is driven by steady, abundant, affordable energy supplies.

So what's wrong with being pro-environment and pro-development? These vital ambitions work symbiotically, and we cannot tolerate one company or industry shutting out or stepping upon another company or industry to inhibit competition. The federal government must remove itself from this arena.

MADE IN AMERICA

The United States has lost millions of manufacturing jobs to foreign nations due to an unfriendly business climate in America and excessive government taxes and regulations. Our citizens can now be the initiators of a huge renaissance in our economy by buying American- made products. Quality and worker productivity are still the hallmarks of American life. With stagnant wages and an abundance of cheap oil and natural gas, the United States could be on the threshold of experiencing a rebound and rebirth in manufacturing and emerging market growth. To improve the business climate we must dramatically reduce government intervention.

Our nation can win back manufacturing jobs through innovation, engineering design, retooling, and developing free market supply chains. Dynamic technology and sourcing techniques will promote an alliance between supply and demand that will also allow foreign companies to be closer to consumers. Providing access, real-time communication and collaboration will allow manufacturers to compete globally by meeting production and time-to-market expectations of cost, quality and delivery.

Rising wages, fuel, and transportation costs, as well as intellectual property risks, are causing companies to reconsider America as a viable manufacturing market. The U.S. is still a huge consumer market, and producers still want to be able to deliver their products quickly and cheaply. New cloud-based systems of technology allow domestic and foreign companies to access the marketplace from anywhere in the world.

NATIONAL DEFENSE

Protecting American lives and defending American soil is the primary purpose and responsibility of the federal government. It will be strengthened by focusing on national interests at home over foreign involvement and trying to police the world. A strong military is strengthened by an armed citizenry and by protecting their rights as set forth in the Bill of Rights.

Foreign aid should be eliminated and the Transportation Safety Administration (TSA) should be reduced in bureaucracy, turned over to the states, or eliminated. Wars will be prevented or won by requiring the President to define victory with a clear mission and strategy and requiring Congress to declare it. Secure borders, economic stability, national unity, and the basic honesty and character of our citizens are all essential to a strong national defense.

To avoid a government takeover of our lives, we must be prepared and be involved. To be prepared, we must have strong families and homes. We should avoid debt and live within our incomes. If every home in America was out of debt and had a supply of food, clothing, and fuel (where possible) we would then be in a position to help others if the need arose. There is wisdom in being prepared.

To be involved, we must understand and defend the Constitution. Being a patriot is not just a good feeling that comes around on the 4th of July. It is a fight for liberty that goes on every day of our lives. Ronald Reagan said:

> *"Freedom is never more than one generation away from extinction. We didn't pass it to our children in the bloodstream. It must be fought for, protected, and handed on for them to do the same, or one day we will spend our sunset years telling our children and our children's children what it was once like in the United States where men were free."*

Too many people believe the fight for liberty and freedom is a battle that has already been won. Some don't understand, and others won't admit, that freedom must be defended every day. Knowing what to do comes with understanding, love, tolerance, and a willingness to fight for what is right.

Today we have too many military bases in too many countries (approximately 900 in 153). To many Americans and others around the world this appears more like building an empire instead of defending our freedom. A strong national defense *does* necessitate some presence on the high seas and in some foreign lands, but we have gone way beyond what is reasonable. I believe our nation should never project weakness. The best way to avoid a fight is to be ready to fight—peace through strength.

Prior to the war in Iraq that began shortly after 9/11, my wife and I got down on our knees and prayed that America would not become involved. The morality behind this war was weak. There was no evidence that Saddam Hussein had directly participated in the tragedy of 9/11. He was certainly guilty of expressing approval of the event, but so were many other nations and peoples. Even if Saddam Hussein had weapons of mass destruction, he had no capability to deploy these weapons against Americans. This war seemed inspired more by resentment. This man we fought in 1990 and drove out of Kuwait with the support of a large international coalition was still in power. Did we allow our national pride to rise above our sense of right and wrong?

Here's the key: Even though I disagreed with the philosophies behind the war, once the United States became engaged, it became my responsibility to support the United States 100 percent. The time for debate was over. Our troops deserved the full commitment of the nation and its citizens. It was imperative to have a goal, a plan, and to execute it to completion.

We can't turn back the clock. I wish that we could, but such sentiments are useless. We must now fight and defeat our enemies whenever and wherever they appear. Like many Americans, I fear they will soon be upon American soil. This is all the more reason to support the 2nd and 4th Amendments of the Constitution.

Consider those who believe the people *should* own guns and those who do not. Among those who believe the public should own guns included George Washington, John Adams, Thomas Jefferson, John Quincy Adams, Abraham Lincoln, Martin Luther King Jr., and Mahatma Gandhi. Among those who believed the people should not own guns are: Napoleon, Adolf Hitler, Joseph Stalin, Mao Ze Dung, Pak Sr. and Jr., and some prominent Americans. The issue is not gun safety. The issue is personal freedom and the ability of citizens to protect themselves against a tyrannical government.

PRISON REFORM

Today America has more people in prison than every other nation on earth combined. This thriving industry has become incomparably corrupt with powerful lobbies helping the system to grow. The industry has become so profitable that it is in the interest of many individuals and industries to continue the status quo and build more prisons and increase the amount of comforts and services. It should offend us all to learn that there are more African Americans currently behind bars in America than were enslaved prior to the Civil War. A congressman who is convicted of drug possession can spend a month in rehab and go back to work. There are approximately 500,000 non-congressmen behind bars for non-violent drug offenses why they are not able to do the same thing.

Once again, the greater part of this problem would resolve itself if we had less government involvement. The crime rate is increasing, and our prisons are becoming increasingly overcrowded. It's been estimated that it costs taxpayers about $35,000 per year for every convict.

For generations, we have heard that "crime doesn't pay". It appears that many people believe crime *does* pay, and there's a good argument to support it. Not only criminals are benefiting from crime. A new prison in your county provides construction jobs and permanent employment for many citizens as well as a tax base for the city, county and state. Do you ever wonder why politicians can be found negotiating over who gets the next prison?

In the end, who really pays for criminal wrongdoing? The answer is that *we* do—you and me and every other citizen. Consumers and taxpayers ultimately pay the expense of all security systems and preventive measures. We also pay the salaries of our law enforcement officers who arrest criminals and bring them to justice. We pay for lawyers in the District Attorney's office who prosecute criminals, along with the judges, juries, and personnel who try and administer cases. Prisoners who are convicted must be housed, fed, clothed, and guarded. Tremendous resources are expended to provide them with comforts as well as aid in their rehabilitation as they serve their time.

Serving time! This phrase is a true oxymoron. Citizens inside and outside of prison both use the phrase "serving time," but who are they serving? They are serving nobody! They are *spending* their time in prison. We can hope they will be rehabilitated in the process, but for the most part prisons have become institutions where inmates recruit and develop skills in crime.

"Serving time" applies to military personnel. Public servants can be described as serving time, but convicts are *spending* time at the expense of the taxpayers. Actually, all citizens who are *not* in prison are serving the prisoners as well as an inmate's family members.

Occasionally, we hear arguments about inmates' rights, including family visits, conjugal visits and comfortable surroundings that include TV etc. We strive to provide them with balanced meals, training, education, and the best medical care. Some have argued that taxpayers should fund alternative medical procedures. It's infinitely easier and quicker for inmates to receive these basic services than for unemployed Americans to apply for and get unemployment insurance. It's often easier for sick prisoners to get healthcare or to pay for needed medication, etc., than for the nation's poor to receive the same benefits. The system often takes care of prisoners more quickly and efficiently. The system serves its criminals better than it serves many people who are homeless or in poverty. The justice behind it all can seem upside down. Rewards and punishment can appear confusing.

One creative entrepreneur suggested contracting with foreign governments to maintain convicted criminals in foreign penitentiaries. Secure facilities could be built and convicts could be fed and clothed, etc., at about 20 percent of the costs that taxpayers currently pay. For example, what would happen if, upon conviction, convicts were immediately transported to an Asian prison and put to use "serving time" in remedial labor functions or even in more sophisticated projects based on their background, abilities, and education? Criminals might think twice if they knew they would be sent to such a prison if they were caught. Escape for non-Asians would be far more difficult, as they would stand out in a crowd and unable to speak the language.

It's a possibility worth considering. Key issues include reducing crime, equal justice under the law, appropriate penalties, and enhanced rehabilitation. The goal is to begin thinking outside the box to resolve a problem that is only growing worse.

THE UNITED NATIONS

There is no justification or advantage for the United States to be involved in the United Nations. We have little to gain and much to lose. The United States gives foreign aid to have other governments finance their U.N. representatives to live in the U.S. and promote a U.N. agenda. The U.N. entangles our foreign diplomats and military forces in projects and offensives in which we have no business becoming involved. The United Nations charter has become one of fostering turmoil around the world and of undermining the sovereignty of the United States. Its silent intent is to have growing global influence, control, and dominion over the U.S. and other nations.

On the surface, the United Nation has many good intentions. However, it is ineffective at accomplishing its goals and fronts other initiatives that appear to be harmful to our country.

Urgent measures need to be made to stop funding the United Nations and help move its headquarters outside of the United States of America. We must also eliminate diplomatic privilege and immunity to UN members, staff, and their dependents. The fact is, today's United Nations is no more effective in accomplishing its original mandate than the original League of Nations founded under President Woodrow Wilson. It does not insure peace and stability. It does not foster a greater sense of cooperation and unity of nations, that in many cases have agendas diametrically opposed to cooperation and unity. It is a forum for many individuals and organizations to weaken the strength of our republic and undermine our national security.

I'm in favor of the UN promoting and administering the non-government organizations (NGOs) that are also non-profit, to help those in need. However, they should do so respecting the sovereignty of nations, not in domination of them.

CHANGING THE NATION'S CAPITAL

I believe our nation's capital is in a congested, outdated, and vulnerable location. To resolve this problem it should be moved. Making such a dynamic statement might cause a few gasps, but I have considered this idea very carefully.

It has been quite obvious for decades that Washington, D.C., has numerous disadvantages and is vulnerable to a multitude of threats. It isn't if, but when these disadvantages will overcome the capital city as now located. It isn't if, but when, domestic or foreign threats will penetrate the bureaucracies and vulnerabilities of Washington, D.C., as it presently stands. Expansive population and tourism growth, along with traffic congestion, have increased the threat from land, sea or air in the District of Columbia.

Article 1, Section 8 of the U.S. Constitution permits the establishment of a district not to exceed 10 miles square that will serve as the nation's seat of government by cession of state land and acceptance by Congress. It was intended that the nation's capital provide for its own maintenance and security. The Residence Act of 1790 approved the creation of the capital on the Potomac River. President George Washington was to select the location of the 100 square miles. On September 9, 1791, the three commissioners overseeing the capital's construction named the city in honor of President Washington. The federal district was named Columbia, which was a poetic name for the United States commonly in use at that time. Congress held its first session in Washington on November 17, 1800.

The federal government agreed to pay for Maryland's and Virginia's remaining war debts in exchange for a new capital in the southern states. In the 1830's, the Virginia side of the Potomac was neglected and ultimately withdrew a section of land in 1846. This left only 6.9 acres on the northern side of the river.

In 1873, following the Civil War, large-scale projects were started in order to modernize the city. However, they bankrupted the District in 1874. Following the New Deal in the 1930's, increased federal spending made it possible to create new buildings, memorials and museums. World War II increased the number of federal employees. The 23rd Amendment granted 3 Electoral College votes to the District of Columbia for president and vice president, but no voting representation in Congress.

Over the years, the financial capital of America migrated from New York City to the legal capital in Washington, D.C. After 1913 an explosive growth in special interests, lobbyists, and law offices dramatically changed the political environment inside and outside the beltway. It was a place of turmoil during the Civil Rights Era. On September 11, 2001, an airliner taken over by foreign terrorists crashed into the Pentagon. Such change and turmoil have caused concern for the integrity, efficiency, and safety of the nation's capital.

Some may question these threats and vulnerabilities. In an age of Intercontinental Ballistic Missiles (ICBMs) and threats of a nuclear holocaust and terrorist attacks some may ask, "How would our capital be any *less* vulnerable in another area of the country?" I believe those in our military would readily admit that with today's military threats, the new reality is that mere minutes and seconds often matter. By necessity, Washington, D.C.,'s present defenses have been inserted in and around existing substructure, often at great complication and cost. I have no doubt that our military planners, admirals, and generals would express enthusiasm about an opportunity to entirely redesign the nation's capital on a clean slate, without the inconveniences of working around existing and congested substructure, and with the opportunity to incorporate the latest technological advances and infrastructure that would eliminate existing gridlock. It would also be an opportunity to introduce some of the most beautiful architectural designs and cityscapes the world has ever seen. Moreover, it would be a tremendous boost to the American economy.

The present District of Columbia would certainly remain a monument to the past 200 years of American history. Its museums and attractions would continue to draw visitors from around the country and around the world.

A new and future capital would provide for increased integrity, efficiency, and safety.

The original capital in Philadelphia was moved to Washington, D.C. to be in the middle of the country and have access to foreign ports. With the country's expansion westward, it is long past the time for our capital to be moved to the heartland of America. It may take more than ten years to complete such a project in stages, but the costs and immediate inconvenience will be far outweighed by the future benefits and savings.

There may be some debate about the exact location in the Midwest, but there can be no justifiable rationale for not having the kind of capital we need at this time in history for our nation.

It's time for a new vision, a fresh beginning. Other emerging economies of the world, such as China and India, have expanded their infrastructures by utilizing regions where none had previously existed. In America's current state of economic distress and political turmoil, we desperately need this kind of fresh and dynamic opportunity. There are at least a dozen ideal locations for new cities that could be built over the next decade or two. This vision must include a new location to house our "seat of government" in an area of the nation that is more centralized, less industrialized, and open to magnificent new changes.

Based on my biased observation and research, the most ideal location would be immediately northeast of Liberty, Missouri. I love the name and it's located near the Kansas City airport and not far from Whitman Air Force Base located between Warrensburg and Sedalia, Missouri. This ten-square-mile district would provide a surrounding buffer zone and allow for state-of-the-art work facilities, housing, and transportation for only the top officials in the three branches of governments. All staff, foreign diplomats, and other parties would be located off-site, with many government agencies remaining in the present Washington, D.C., area.

Again, it's time for a fresh clear vision and a new beginning.

Chapter 15

A View of Greatness

CLOSING STATEMENTS

What I have presented in the previous chapters is only an overview—a brief glimpse—of my vision and plans after I am elected President of the United States. What America lacks today is true vision—brave new ideas that will preserve our Constitution while transforming our economy and renewing our pride as citizens of the greatest nation in history.

Let's stop rehashing the old problems that have been perpetually recycled for more than a generation. We have created a system whose very survival depends upon preserving growing bureaucracies. Undoubtedly these bureaucracies will fight tooth and nail to justify their existence and, perhaps, even to expand government power wherever possible.

As I have already stated several times, the solutions to our nation's problems can be solved with common sense. In fact, the themes of my campaign would highlight these two "C" words—*Constitution* and *Common Sense*. But these aren't the only themes. Transformation, Modernization, and Restoration would also be a part of it. Popular politicians run their campaigns based upon another "C" word—*Change*. I could easily offer this as a third theme in my own campaign. However, I believe many have altered the meaning of this word into a kind of change that seeks to overrule or destroy many of the values so carefully—and prayerfully—established by our Founders. Therefore, I must select the theme of "Restoration" in order for voters to know that my vision involves change, but such changes will focus upon restoring the values that made this republic possible in the first place.

America must again be reminded that freedom and liberty are fragile things, and that if we are not willing to fight to keep them in place, they will inevitably be lost to history, waiting in limbo for another people—another nation—with the courage and fortitude to cobble together the blueprint that was America. However, the climate and conditions—both political and religious—that conjoined to create the circumstances that made something like America possible may be so rare and unique that I fear any other attempt to recreate what we now have on hand may be futile. It is far better to fight to preserve what we currently have.

In this book I have offered readers a glimpse of my background and history, my political perspectives, and my visions for the future. I hope more than anything that *Dark Horse Candidate* has presented readers with an honest perspective of who I am as a person. As I've said before, I believe integrity is the most important quality that any politician should possess—most of all the President of the United States. I invite everyone to examine, explore and dissect my words, as well as ask a myriad of additional questions, so I will become better known to the American public. In the end, it's *you* who must make the final judgment regarding who I am and what I have to say.

Some of the ideas I have presented here are vital to our future success. Some ideas are entirely new, but I believe they are all vital. Some concepts may even be alarming, but I'm convinced this is only because they *are* so new, and no one is presenting such solutions in the same manner. My sincere hope is that my ideas will enlarge your imagination, stimulate and swell your feelings of patriotism, and aid in your ability to envision the same possibilities for America that I envision. Our greatness cannot spring from a vision of America that does not include the blood, sacrifice, and intellectual struggle of our Founding Fathers. In the sweltering heat of 1787, they produced a document unrivaled in the history of the world.

To love America is to love the Constitution of the United States and to pledge allegiance to it, and to our flag, and to our republic. Other nations have flags, land, history, culture, traditions and wonderful people. But only the United States of America has the Constitution that defines us as "one nation under God." We are the one nation with the status of being the oldest republic still flourishing upon the face of the earth. I love America. My desire is to serve her and to serve all Americans. Join with me and focus our efforts toward saving the Constitution and getting our nation on the right path – on the "Patriot's Path". I take the distinction between *statesman* and *politician* very seriously. My ideas, policies and actions would ever reject calling myself a politician. Instead, I would elevate the term statesman and define my campaign and my Presidency by its ideals.

My ambition is to become the first true *citizen* President of the United States. I owe no political favors to any particular lobby or constituency. Although I run as a Republican, my objective is to do my best to bring Americans together in a way that no president has managed to do in modern history, with the possible exception of Ronald Reagan, who carried 49 of 50 states when he ran for re-election in 1984.

So, let the race begin and let the examination of my platform and my character begin. I will devote all of my time toward trumpeting these ideals and policies while continually pointing beyond myself toward the Constitution and Common Sense.

May God bless this nation, and bless the President who serves in its highest office. I would be honored to take that role, and I would devote every particle of energy inside me to fulfilling my promises for a better America. I will always to be an American and I will continue to fight for the principles that made America great. Nothing will change that burning desire within me. It's a fight I intend to carry on until my last breath. I know that we are not alone. My goal is to inspire all other Americans who feel the same and gain their attention and support. If we come together with a common purpose, we cannot be overcome—no matter the problem, no matter the struggle, no matter the enemy.

I invite all Americans to allow me, Dale Christensen, the Dark Horse Candidate, to become the President who can finally bring Americans together in a common purpose, and forever place the ideals of liberty, freedom, and equality upon the highest platforms ever erected by mankind.

A GLIMPSE OF GREATNESS

In a late-evening English class my wife and I recently taught in Connecticut, I met Madeline Mosquera. She came with her grandmother, who was struggling to learn English. I told Madeline that someday she could achieve her dreams and even become President of the United States. My six-year-old friend excitedly told me she wanted to be the first lady president. I asked her to write her name and her dream on a piece of paper.

I want to share this with you so you can help Madeline achieve her dream.

> Madeline
> Mosquera
> I want to be the
> president.

One with the American Dream

What's happening to the USA?

Need for a Dark Horse Candidate

Footnotes

Chapter 1

Hafen, Mary Ann S. "Life Story." TMs [microfilm], 4, The Church of Jesus Christ of Latter-day Saints, Historical Department, Library-Archives Division, Salt Lake City; Mulder, *Mormons from Scandinavia,* 238.

Jensen, *History of the Scandinavian Mission,* 148; Fjeld, *A Brief History of the Fjeld-Fields Family,* 17.

Astle, [Diary], *An Enduring Legacy* 10:107; Church Emigration, 1860. Church of Jesus Christ of Latter-day Saints, Historical Department, Library-Archives Division, Salt Lake City. See also Memmott, Thomas. *Thomas Memmott Journal,* vol. 1, ed. by H. Kirk Memmott (privately printed, 1976), 45. It was quite common to bury the dead soon after they passed away.

Church Emigration, 1860; Fjeld, [Autobiography], *A Brief History of the Fjeld-Fields Family,* 18.

Jaques, John, [Letter], *Latter-day Saints Millennial Star* 18:26 (June 28, 1856), 412.

Zobell, *His Story,* 49-50.

Jaques, [Letter], *Latter-day Saints Millennial Star* 18:26 (May 29, 1856), 413.

Jones, D., [Letter], *Latter-day Saints Millennial Star* 18:27 (July 5, 1856), 428.

Larrabee, [Autobiography], *Our Pioneer Heritage,* comp. by Kate B. Carter, vol. 12 (Salt Lake City: Daughters of Utah Pioneers, 1969), 197.

Chapter 10

Ferrand, Max, Ed. *Records of the Federal Convention of 1787,* vol. 1. New Haven, CT: Yale University Press, 1937. Pg. 155, 407.

Federalist Papers, Number 45. Pg. 287-288.

Rossum, Ralph A. "California and the Seventeenth Amendment." Ed. Janiskee, Brian P. and Masugi, Ken. *The California Republic.* Lanham, MD: Rowman & Littlefield, 2004. Pg. 70-71.

Federalist Papers, Number 62, Pg. 377.

Federalist Papers, Number 10, Pg. 76.

Congressional Record. 53, 1894. 7775.

Senator Zell Miller, *Congressional Record.* 24 Apr. 2004: S4503

Holcombe, Randall G. "The Growth of the Federal Government in the 1920s." *Cato Journal.* Vol. 16, No. 2. Fall 1996. Pg. 175-177.

Rossum, Ralph A., *Federalism, the Supreme Court, and the Seventeenth Amendment: The Irony of Constitutional Democracy.* Lanham, MD: Lexington Books, 2001. Pg. 281.